The
Rhode Island Colony

by Dennis B. Fradin

Consultant: Sukey Lutman
Reference Librarian
Rhode Island Historical Society

 CHILDRENS PRESS ®
CHICAGO

Library of Congress Cataloging-in-Publication Data

Fradin, Dennis B.
    The Rhode Island colony / by Dennis B. Fradin.
        p.   cm.
    Includes index.
    Summary: Traces the history of Rhode Island to 1790 when it became the
last colony to ratify the Constitution.
    ISBN 0-516-00391-7
    1. Rhode Island—History—Colonial period, ca. 1600-1775—Juvenile
literature. 2. Rhode Island—History—Colonial period, ca. 1600-1775—
Biography—Juvenile literature. 3. Rhode Island—History—Revolution, 1775-
1783—Juvenile literature. 4. Rhode Island—History—Revolution, 1775-1783—
Biography—Juvenile literature. 5. Rhode Island—Biography—Juvenile
literature. [1. Rhode Island—History—Colonial period, ca. 1600-1775.
2. Rhode Island—History—Revolution, 1775-1783.] I. Title.
F82.F73   1989
974.5′02—dc19   89-744
                                                                                 CIP
                                                                                 AC

Table of Contents

View of the city of Providence as it appeared in 1808

Chapter I

Introducing the Ocean State

*Road-Island is of a considerable bigness, and justly
called THE GARDEN OF NEW ENGLAND, for its
Fertility and Pleasantness. It abounds with all
Things necessary for the life of Man, is excellent for
Sheep, Kine [cows], and Horses; and being
environed by the Sea, it is freed from the dangers of
Bears, Wolves, and Foxes. . . .*

> *Description of Rhode Island by an
> unknown writer in 1690*

Rhode Island is the state with the smallest area
and the longest official name. Covering just 1,210
square miles, Rhode Island could fit inside
average-sized Illinois more than forty-five times.
Nearly 500 Rhode Islands could be squeezed into
Alaska, the largest state.

Rhode Island is located in the northeastern
United States, in the region called *New England*.
The other five New England states are Maine, New
Hampshire, Vermont, Massachusetts, and
Connecticut. Rhode Island is bounded by the
Atlantic Ocean to the south, Massachusetts to the
east and north, and Connecticut to the west.

Map of the
thirteen colonies

The Old Town House on the corner of Benefit and College streets in Providence, once served as the town hall and police station. It was first built for the First Congregational Church.

Map of Rhode Island

Narragansett Bay, an inlet of the Atlantic Ocean, extends inland about two-thirds up eastern Rhode Island.

Although it is called Rhode Island for short, the smallest state's official name is *State of Rhode Island and Providence Plantations*. Back in the 1630s, some people settled on Rhode Island's mainland, which was called *Providence* Plantations. Others settled on the Island of Rhode Island (the largest of the thirty-six islands that belong to the state). The mainland and island

6

settlements later joined to form the Colony of Rhode Island and Providence Plantations. When the United States broke away from Britain in the late 1700s, Rhode Island became the *State of* rather than the *Colony of* Rhode Island and Providence Plantations.

Rhode Island has two main nicknames. Because of its size, it has long been called *Little Rhody*. Because it lies along the Atlantic Ocean, Rhode Island is officially nicknamed the *Ocean State*. Providence is Rhode Island's capital and largest city. The Ocean State's other major cities include Warwick, Cranston, Pawtucket, Woonsocket, and Newport.

Rhode Island was one of England's Thirteen American Colonies, along with Virginia, Massachusetts, New Hampshire, New York, Connecticut, Maryland, Delaware, Pennsylvania, North Carolina, New Jersey, South Carolina, and Georgia. Rhode Island was first colonized by Massachusetts people who were seeking a place where they could worship as they chose. The first English settlement in Rhode Island was founded in 1636 by Roger Williams, an Englishman who had fled Massachusetts to escape religious persecution. Williams named his new settlement

Providence and made it the first American town to guarantee freedom of worship to everyone. Anne Hutchinson and other Massachusetts people who were looking for a religious haven soon built several other towns in Rhode Island.

When the Rhode Island towns united into a single colony in 1644, freedom of religion was extended to all its people. In fact, during the early years of American colonization, Rhode Island offered the greatest amount of religious freedom of any colony. England also granted Rhode Island the most self-government of the Thirteen Colonies.

The Touro Synagogue in Newport, Rhode Island was built in 1762.

Yet during the Revolutionary War era, when the colonies were breaking away from Britain to become the United States, Rhode Islanders were among the first to rebel. In 1765 a mob in Newport, Rhode Island, burned a boat belonging to the British ship *Maidstone*. This was one of the first violent acts against the British in the years leading up to the revolution. Four years later, in another early act of rebellion, Rhode Islanders burned the British warship *Liberty*. When war with Britain seemed inevitable, Rhode Island was the first of the Thirteen Colonies to declare itself independent of British rule.

During the Revolutionary War (1775–1783) several thousand soldiers and sailors from Rhode Island fought on the American side. Rhode Island also produced several important leaders, among them the great General Nathanael Greene and Esek Hopkins, first Commander in Chief of the United States Navy.

Although Rhode Island had been the leader in declaring its independence from Britain, it was the last of the Thirteen Colonies to become a state under the United States Constitution. Afraid of being swallowed up by the larger states, Rhode Island did not even send delegates to the convention that created the Constitution in 1787.

Pulpit of Trinity Church in Newport, Rhode Island

Pawtucket Falls about 1789

Finally, in a very close vote, Rhode Island became the thirteenth state by approving the U.S. Constitution on May 29, 1790.

The little state with the long name has contributed a great deal to the country since the colonial era. About the time of Rhode Island's statehood, a Pawtucket man named Samuel Slater helped found the textile (cloth-making) industry, which began the Industrial Revolution in the United States. Several years later two brothers, Nehemiah and Seril Dodge of Providence, founded the jewelry industry in America. Today jewelry and textiles are still important Rhode Island products. Machinery, silverware, rubber and plastic goods, electronic equipment, foods, and ships are among the other products made in the Ocean State.

Considering its size, Rhode Island has also produced a large number of famous people. A few well-known Rhode Islanders of colonial times are described later in this book. Famous Rhode Islanders of the years since statehood include the portrait artist Gilbert Stuart (1755–1828) who was born in North Kingstown, and the U.S. Navy hero Oliver Hazard Perry (1785–1819) who was born in South Kingstown. Prudence Crandall (1803–1890), a famous teacher who worked for the rights of black people, was born in Hopkinton, Rhode Island. Providence was the birthplace of songwriter George M. Cohan (1878–1942), one of the most famous names in American theater.

Gilbert Stuart

Rhode Island has done a remarkable job of preserving the homes of its famous citizens of the past. Each year thousands of people visit Rhode Island to see its historic houses, churches, and other buildings dating back to colonial times. The Ocean State also attracts crowds of vacationers who come to sail, swim, and fish along its picturesque Atlantic Coast.

Oliver Hazard Perry

Algonquian women build a family lodge.

Chapter II

The Indians of Rhode Island

Boast not, proud English, of thy birth and blood, Thy brother Indian is by birth as good.

Roger Williams, writing in the 1640s

Prehistoric tools and other remains discovered in the area reveal that people have lived in Rhode Island for at least 8,000 years. The early Indians hunted deer with stone-tipped spears. The deer provided them with food and clothing. They also gathered clams and other shellfish along Narragansett Bay. However, little is known about the customs, beliefs, and ways of life of the early Rhode Islanders.

By the early 1600s, about 10,000 Indians belonging to modern tribes lived in what is now Rhode Island. The main tribes were the Narragansett, the Wampanoag, the Niantic, the Nipmuc, and the Pequot. These tribes all belonged to the Algonquian Indian family, who lived throughout much of what are now the eastern United States and eastern Canada.

Painting of an
Niantic Indian

Occupying the Narragansett Bay region, the Narragansetts were the only major tribe to live almost wholly within Rhode Island. They were also Rhode Island's most powerful tribe. Of the 10,000 Indians in Rhode Island in the early 1600s, perhaps half of them were Narragansetts.

The other tribes, making up the remaining 5,000 people, all lived across the borders in what are now Rhode Island's neighboring states. The Wampanoags dwelled mainly in southeastern Massachusetts but also occupied present-day

Bristol County in eastern Rhode Island. The Niantics made their homes in southwestern Rhode Island and southeastern Connecticut. The Nipmucs lived in southern Massachusetts and northern Rhode Island and Connecticut. The Pequots lived mainly in southeastern Connecticut but spilled over into southwestern Rhode Island.

Since the Indians traveled a great deal by canoe and loved to fish, they generally built their villages near bodies of water. They lived in huts called *wigwams*, which were made of wooden poles covered by tree bark, reed mats, or animal skins.

Rhode Island has a great deal of fertile ground, especially around Narragansett Bay. The Rhode Island tribes were excellent farmers. The women grew the food crops, consisting mainly of corn, beans, and squash. Several dozen women often worked together to plant and harvest their crops. The men grew tobacco, which was smoked in religious ceremonies and used to treat toothaches!

Besides farming, the Indian tribes obtained food by gathering, hunting, and fishing. The women gathered many kinds of roots and berries. The men did the hunting and fishing. They killed deer, birds, and other animals with spears and bows and arrows. They fished in Narragansett

Tools used to grind corn.

Woven Indian basket

15

Bay and in Rhode Island rivers with nets, spears, and bone hooks.

The women cooked the vegetables, meat, and fish into tasty soups and stews. One popular dish among the East Coast Indians was made by cooking corn and beans together. The Narragansetts called this dish *msekwatas*, but the white colonists of later times called it succotash. The Rhode Island Indians also enjoyed a bread made of cornmeal and crushed strawberries.

Although some important men in the tribes had several wives, most families consisted of a father, mother, and children. The children learned how to do things by working alongside their parents. Girls learned to cook, sew, and farm by helping their mothers. Boys learned to hunt, fish, and

Fire was used to cook food and to make canoes.

make canoes by helping their fathers. Indian
parents were generally very tender toward their
children, and most children were respectful of
their elders. However, Roger Williams, the founder
of the Rhode Island Colony, reported that some
young Rhode Island Indians were what we would
call "spoiled brats."

The Rhode Island Indians had no written
language, paper, or metal. Yet they found ways to
keep count, pay for goods, and send messages.
They used corn kernels to count up to a hundred
thousand. Like other Native Americans along the
Atlantic Ocean, the Rhode Island Indians made

Wampum belt

wampum—polished white and purple shell beads. The wampum was used as money, but was also at times strung onto belts in picture form. The pictures recorded tribal history or were used to send picture messages from one tribe or person to another. The word *wampum* comes from the Narragansett word *wampompeag*, meaning a string of white shell beads. Another Narragansett word that the English adopted was *sachima*, referring to the chief, or leader, of the tribe. The English who arrived in the 1600s changed the word slightly to *sachem*.

In religious matters, the Indians greatly differed from the Europeans on the other side of the Atlantic Ocean. Although they argued over religion, nearly all Europeans worshiped one god. The Indians felt that the woods, rivers, and sky were filled with many gods. Throughout the year they held religious festivals to honor their deities.

The men smoked tobacco at these festivals in the belief that the smoke carried their prayers up to the gods.

The Indians also enjoyed games and sports. Along the coastal beaches they played a kind of football game in which the goals were as much as a mile apart. Sometimes one village played another in these football games. The Indians also held running and swimming contests, and the men liked to gamble with dice made of plum pits.

When English colonists arrived in Rhode Island in the 1630s, the Indians generally welcomed them, provided them with food, and helped them survive. At first the colonists were grateful for the help. Later, however, the colonists began taking more and more Indian land, and the tribes were forced to fight them. The result was that thousands of the Indians were killed or enslaved. Today Rhode Island is home to only about 3,000 Indians, some of whom are descended from the region's precolonial Indian tribes.

Historians believe Leif Eriksson landed on the shores of North America long before Columbus sailed to the New World.

Chapter III

Exploration and First Colonists

Why have you come here?

> *A question the Indians kept asking the first Rhode Island colonists*

EXPLORATION

The identity of the first European to explore the present-day United States is unknown. For generations, schoolchildren believed that Christopher Columbus "discovered America" in 1492. But Columbus never reached what is now the United States. Moreover, a number of Europeans may have reached the present-day United States long before 1492. Vikings (Norwegians and other Scandinavians) are known to have sailed to North America beginning with Leif Eriksson's voyage in about the year 1000. With his followers, Eriksson landed somewhere in what is now New England or eastern Canada.

Old Stone Mill

A few scattered relics have been found that the Vikings may have left behind during their early voyages to North America. The Old Stone Mill in Newport, Rhode Island, is a 26-foot-tall circular tower that may have been built by the Vikings in about the year 1000. However, because of colonial relics that have been unearthed nearby, most historians think that the tower actually dates from the 1600s. They think it was probably built by Rhode Island governor Benedict Arnold, ancestor of the famed Revolutionary War traitor of the same name. Even if the tower was built in the 1600s, it is still possible that Vikings visited the Rhode Island region hundreds of years earlier.

If the Vikings never reached Rhode Island, the Portuguese sailor Miguel de Cortereal may have been the first to explore the state's coastal regions in the early 1500s. Cortereal is thought to have been shipwrecked on the New England coast in 1502 and to have spent several years exploring the region and living with the Indians. One clue about this is an inscription on Dighton Rock, a granite boulder located in southeastern Massachusetts not far from Providence, Rhode Island. Translated from Latin, the words on the rock read "M. Cortereal 1511 by God's grace the leader of the Indians." Exactly where Miguel de Cortereal explored and lived remains a mystery.

The first European known to have explored present-day Rhode Island was Giovanni da Verrazano, an Italian who sailed for the king of France. In early 1524 Verrazano voyaged westward on the *Dauphine* in the hope of finding a short route to Asia. Instead, he arrived at Cape Fear, North Carolina, and then turned northward. Verrazano sailed all the way north to the Canadian coast just beyond Maine. Along the way, he became the first known European to explore the coasts of what are now several Mid-Atlantic and New England states, including Rhode Island.

Giovanni da Verrazano

Verrazano's ship explored
Newport Harbor.

During the time he spent in the Rhode Island region, Verrazano explored Narragansett Bay. When he returned to France, he described his voyage for the king. Among other things, he wrote that a triangular island in the Narragansett Bay area reminded him of the island of Rhodes in the Aegean Sea. Verrazano's reference to the island of Rhodes is usually considered the source for the name of the colony of Rhode Island.

However, some historians think that the Dutchman Adriaen Block coined the name Rhode Island. In 1613, aboard the *Tiger*, Block came to the New York region, which was then claimed by the Dutch. After trading with the Indians for furs, Block anchored off Manhattan Island, which is now part of New York City. Somehow the *Tiger* caught fire and was destroyed, but Block and his crew were able to swim to Manhattan Island. The men might have died if left on their own, but some friendly Indians helped them build cabins where they passed the winter of 1613–1614. Block and his men are thought to have been the first Europeans to live in what is now New York City.

In spring of 1614, Block and his men cut down trees and built a new ship, the *Onrust (Restless)*. The *Onrust* wasn't big enough to attempt the difficult Atlantic crossing, so Block used it to do a little exploring. Captain Block and his men sailed up the Connecticut River, claiming Connecticut for The Netherlands. They also explored the Rhode Island region, where they were fed and kindly treated by the Indians.

Block noticed that an island in Narragansett Bay had red clay along its shore. Because of this, Block called it *Roodt Eylandt*, meaning "Red

Island" in Dutch. This may have inspired people to start calling the region Rhode Island. Or perhaps Verrazano's *island of Rhodes* comment and Block's *Roodt Eylandt* reference combined to inspire the name.

In any case, an island and later the whole colony became known as Rhode Island. A major bridge in Rhode Island is named after Verrazano, and Block Island is named for the Dutch explorer and trader Adriaen Block.

FIRST COLONISTS

To understand why colonists first came to Rhode Island, it helps to know about conditions in England and in Massachusetts in the early 1600s. Freedom of religion did not exist in England at that time. Many thousands of people who refused to follow the teachings of the Church of England were stripped of their property and often jailed. Some English people escaped persecution by going to America to live. Massachusetts was first colonized by such people.

In late 1620 the Pilgrims, a religious group that had completely separated from the Church of England, arrived in what is now southeastern Massachusetts. There they built the first permanent English settlement—the Plymouth

Colony. About ten years later a group called the Puritans arrived in the same region. Instead of leaving the Church of England, however, the Puritans tried to improve it from within by simplifying services and focusing more on the Bible. The Puritans settled to the north of the Pilgrims and founded the Massachusetts Bay Colony.

When the Puritans first came to Massachusetts, an Englishman named William Blackstone was living alone in a cottage at a place since named Boston's Beacon Hill. Blackstone, who had come to Massachusetts several years earlier, was something of a hermit who liked to read and tend his orchards. After hearing that the Puritans needed a place to settle, Blackstone invited them to come live near him. Hundreds of Puritans did so, and built the town of Boston, Massachusetts, around his home.

Blackstone's house

Both the Pilgrims and the Puritans had come to the New World because of religious persecution. Once in America, however, some of them in turn persecuted people who disagreed with them. The Puritans especially felt that God had chosen them to show everyone how to worship. A number of people who opposed Puritan teachings were either forced out of Massachusetts by the Puritans or left of their own accord. Some of these refugees from Massachusetts founded the first towns in Rhode Island.

The first known English colonist to come to Rhode Island was William Blackstone, the very man who had been so kind to the Puritans at Boston. Partly because the area was getting too crowded for him and partly because he opposed Puritan teachings, in 1635 Blackstone moved about fifty miles southwest of Boston into present-day Rhode Island. A few miles north of where the Rhode Island town of Cumberland now stands, near a river later named for him, William Blackstone built a farm called Study Hill. He planted a garden and an apple orchard, resumed his reading, and later worked as a preacher after other colonists arrived.

Blackstone, who had been Boston's first colonist, thus became the first colonist in Rhode Island. But he is not considered the founder of the Rhode Island Colony for two reasons. First, he did nothing to build a colony. Second, although the land where Blackstone lived is part of Rhode Island today, it belonged to Massachusetts until 1747. The person honored as "the founder of Rhode Island" was the remarkable Roger Williams.

The London-born Williams had an idea that made him a misfit in England. The young

William Blackstone

minister believed that all people had the right to worship as they pleased. Since he and many others could not do this in England, Williams decided to sail to America with his wife. After a voyage of almost ten weeks, Roger and Mary Williams reached Boston, Massachusetts, in February 1631.

Between 1631 and 1635 Roger Williams worked as a preacher in several Massachusetts towns. He had a strong desire to learn more about the Indians and spent a great deal of time eating and talking with them in their wigwams. Few European-born people in the history of the Thirteen Colonies were as well-liked by the Indians as Roger Williams. In fact, he got along better with the Indians than he did with many Massachusetts officials.

Roger Williams

Roger Williams disagreed with the Puritan leaders on several important matters. For one thing, he was still teaching that all people should be allowed to worship as they pleased. For another, he pointed out the astounding (but true) fact that the English were cheating the Indians out of their land.

Because the laws and government in Massachusetts were based on religion, those who disagreed with the Puritan religious leaders were considered lawbreakers. Roger Williams was brought to trial several times for what Massachusetts officials called his "dangerous opinions." He did not stop expressing those opinions, even after being warned to do so. In October 1635 Williams was ordered to leave Massachusetts. Since winter was approaching, he was allowed to remain until spring—as long as he kept his strange ideas to himself during his last months in the colony.

Massachusetts officials soon learned that Williams had expressed his "dangerous opinions" to guests invited to his house in Salem, a few miles northeast of Boston. In January 1636 a warrant was sent to Roger Williams' house, ordering him to go to Boston immediately, where he was to be placed on a ship bound for England. Williams refused to leave his home, and soon learned that armed men were coming to seize him and see that he was sent back to England.

Roger and Mary Williams had lived in America for five years and did not want to leave this new land. Besides, Mary had recently given birth to a daughter named Freeborn Williams, and the family was in no condition for ocean travel.

Engraving showing Roger Williams leaving his family in Salem.

During his difficulties in Massachusetts, Williams had considered building a settlement near Narragansett Bay, in present-day Rhode Island. Now that he had to leave Massachusetts, he decided that the Narragansett shore was the place to make a new home for his family and his followers.

Roger Williams told his wife to remain in Salem with their two daughters, Mary and Freeborn, until he sent for them. Then on a cold January day in 1636 he set out from his home in Salem, Massachusetts, toward Narragansett Bay. His exact route is not known, but it is thought that he traveled partly by boat and partly on foot. After several days of heading south through the frozen countryside, Williams reached a Wampanoag Indian village on the east side of Narragansett Bay, where Warren, Rhode Island, now stands.

The Wampanoag Indians welcomed the weary Roger Williams. Their leader was Chief Massasoit, who had befriended the Pilgrims at Plymouth, and who with about ninety of his people had been invited to the Pilgrims' famous Thanksgiving feast in fall of 1621. Massasoit and his people shared their wigwams and food with Roger Williams and made him feel at home. All his life, Williams would remember that he had received

The Indians sheltered Roger Williams.

more kindness from the Indians than he had from his own people.

Roger Williams bought some land at what is now East Providence, Rhode Island, from Massasoit. With a few other outcasts from Massachusetts, Williams moved there and began building a settlement. The refugees had already planted their crops and started building their houses when Williams received bad news from his friend Edward Winslow, the Plymouth Colony governor. The spot where Williams and his followers were settling was claimed by Plymouth. Governor Winslow did not mind if they settled on Plymouth land. However, he was worried that the more powerful Massachusetts Bay Colony would be angry if the Plymouth Colony provided refuge for Williams. Governor Winslow asked that Williams and his followers move beyond the lands claimed by Plymouth.

In June 1636 the little group went a short way west of their original settlement to an area claimed by the Narragansett Indians. Roger Williams obtained land from the two main Narragansett chiefs, Canonicus and his nephew Miantonomo. On this land Williams and his companions began building a town.

Williams called his town *Providence*—a word referring to God's guidance. He chose that name because he felt God had provided the place for him and other victims of religious persecution. As Providence was the first non-Indian town to be built in Rhode Island, Roger Williams is honored as the founder of the Rhode Island Colony. Under his guidance, Providence became the first American town to offer complete freedom of religion.

At first Williams and his handful of followers built some huts similar to the Indians' wigwams. The settlers had arrived too late in the year to plant crops, but there were plenty of shellfish around Narragansett Bay and plenty of animals to be hunted in the nearby forests. The Indians also shared some of their corn and beans with the newcomers.

Roger Williams soon sent for Mary and his two children. He also sent out word that Providence was a haven for people of all religious views. The little settlement began attracting other Massachusetts people who had suffered from religious persecution. Within a short time Providence was home to several dozen people, the huts were replaced by sturdier houses, and streets were laid out in Rhode Island's first town.

ROGER WILLIAMS (1603?-1683)

Roger Williams was born in London in the early 1600s, but the exact year is unknown. He lived with his family in a building that also housed his father's tailor shop. Little is known about Roger's early life, so we don't know why or when he developed his ideas about freedom of religion. He may have been influenced by a gruesome event that occurred in London when he was about nine years old.

In spring of 1612, not far from Roger's home, a man was burned at the stake for holding unpopular religious views. Even if Roger did not witness the burning of this living human being, he certainly heard people talking about it. From his later writings, it is apparent that by his teens Roger held unusual religious views himself. He later wrote that his parents, who belonged to the Church of England, "persecuted" him for years because of his beliefs.

Young Roger read a great deal, especially the Bible, and also learned a method of rapid writing called shorthand. He probably would have missed out on a higher education were it not for Sir Edward Coke, an elderly lawyer and judge who was impressed by the teenager. Roger went to court with Sir Edward and took down the proceedings in shorthand for him. Thanks to the London lawyer, Roger went to school on a scholarship and later was admitted to Cambridge University. He was graduated in 1627, and soon after he was ordained as a minister.

In 1629 Roger became chaplain to a wealthy country family. Late that same year he married Mary Barnard, with whom he was to live happily for many years and raise a large family in a distant land. After living in England for the first year of their marriage, the couple decided to move to the New World. Roger thought that in America he would be able to express the unusual religious views he was developing, and he also hoped to convert the Indians to Christianity.

Roger and Mary Williams sailed on the *Lyon* in late 1630, and reached Boston in February 1631 after a stormy two-month voyage. It was in the New World that Roger Williams accomplished the things that made him famous.

Two of Roger Williams' most remarkable qualities were his kindness and his fairness. He harbored no grudge against the Massachusetts people who had forced him to leave, and he tried to keep the peace between them and the Indians. He also tried to protect the Indians from the colonists. One of the few bitter disputes he had was with a colonist who wanted to defraud the Indians out of a great deal of land.

About three years after founding Providence, Roger Williams became a Seeker—one who believed in Christianity without belonging to a church.

Williams accomplished a great deal in the many years of life that remained to him. He wrote and spoke about liberty and conscience, served as president of the Rhode Island Colony, and remained active until almost the end of his life. In 1672, at about the age of 70, Williams rowed over twenty miles to Newport where he debated several Quakers. Although he did not do any fighting, he was nearly 75 when he served as a soldier during King Philip's War. This great man, who taught that "the peacemakers are Sons of God" and who always promoted "justice and mercy," died at about the age of 80 in the colony he had helped to found.

Roger Williams building his cabin

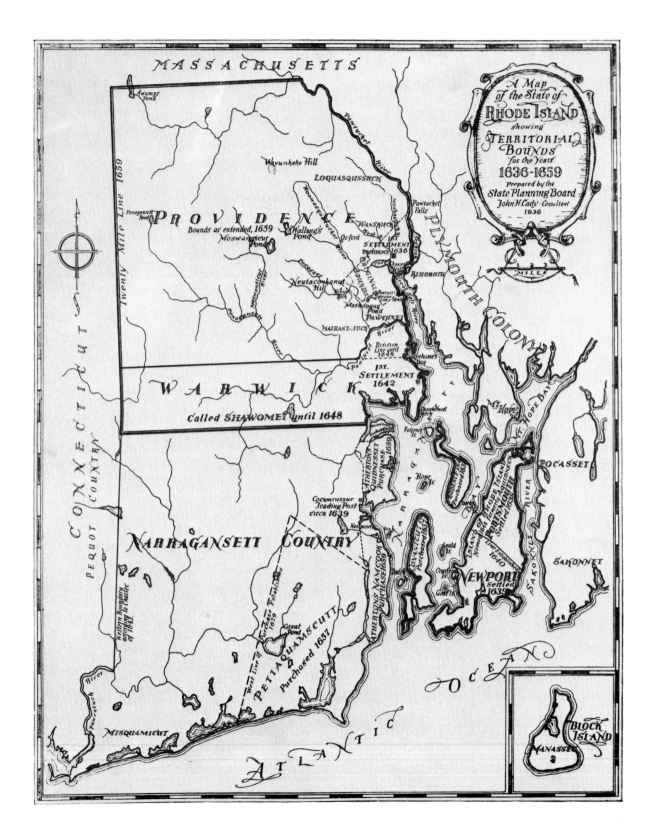

Chapter IV

The Colony's Early Years: 1636-1660

The most wise God hath provided and cut out this part of the world [Rhode Island] for a refuge and receptacle for all sorts of consciences.

> *John Haynes, Connecticut governor, to Roger Williams*

Rhode Island . . . is the receptacle of all sorts of riff-raff people and it is nothing else than the sewer of New England.

> *From a letter written by two Dutch ministers of New York during the Rhode Island Colony's early years*

Because Williams was fair and friendly toward the Indians, the tribes loved him. However, many other American colonists cheated the Indians out of their lands and were otherwise cruel to them. Connecticut's Pequot tribe developed an especially strong hatred for the colonists. Soon after the English colonists began building permanent settlements in Connecticut in 1633, the Pequots began raiding those settlements.

The people of Providence knew that the Pequots posed a threat to them, too, because just fifty miles separated the new town from the Pequots' Connecticut villages. The situation became even more dangerous when the Pequots asked the Narragansetts, who had previously been their enemies, to help them drive the colonists out of New England.

In 1636 Pequot messengers visited the two main Narragansett chiefs, Canonicus and Miantonomo, with the intention of winning them over to their side. Massachusetts officials learned about this, and asked Roger Williams to help prevent the Narragansetts from aiding the Pequots. For the sake of his brand-new town of Providence and the other New England colonies, Williams crossed Narragansett Bay by canoe and went to Canonicus's lodge, where the Pequots were still talking to the Narragansetts. Speaking in their language, Roger Williams convinced his Narragansett friends to side with the English against the Pequots. By doing this, Williams probably saved the lives of many colonists.

The Narragansetts' decision turned out to be disastrous for the Pequots. In addition to the Narragansetts, a branch of the Pequots called the Mohegans also fought on the English side during

Roger Williams pleads with Canonicus.

the Pequot War, which was fought in 1637. The Pequots had no chance against the combined forces of the colonists, the Narragansetts, and the Mohegans.

At dawn of June 5, 1637, an army of Connecticut and Massachusetts colonists with their Narragansett and Mohegan allies attacked a large Pequot village in what is now southeastern Connecticut, near the Rhode Island border. The Pequots in the village had only bows and arrows and tomahawks, while the colonial army had guns. Led by Captain John Mason of Connecticut, the colonial army set fire to the Pequots' village, burning to death nearly all of the 700 Pequot men, women, and children there. This vicious massacre virtually destroyed the Pequots as a tribe. Although he was praised for convincing the Narragansetts to side with the colonists, Roger Williams was upset that his Narragansett friends had taken part in the slaughter of the Pequots.

Providence remained Rhode Island's only English settlement for just two years. While the Providence settlers were building their new town, a woman named Anne Hutchinson was having troubles in Massachusetts similar to those Roger Williams had experienced several years earlier. Anne Hutchinson differed with the Puritan ministers on various important matters. For one thing, at religious meetings held in her Boston home she said that people could contact God without the help of a minister. For another, she thought that salvation was possible through faith alone.

In 1637 Anne Hutchinson was tried for disagreeing with church officials and ordered to leave Massachusetts. Since it was late in the year, she was allowed to remain in Massachusetts until

Anne Hutchinson leaves the Massachusetts Colony.

the weather turned warmer—provided that she keep her ideas to herself. Like Roger Williams, Anne Hutchinson continued to express her views. For this she was expelled from the Puritan Church in early 1638. No Puritans were allowed to have anything more to do with her, and she was ordered to leave Massachusetts within a few days.

By spring of 1638 Anne and William Hutch-inson and their children, along with several friends, had come to Rhode Island. On Roger Williams' advice, the refugees built a settlement on Aquidneck Island. Williams was always careful about making fair deals with the Indians for their land. He arranged for the newcomers to pay Canonicus and Miantonomo a large amount of wampum for the land on Aquidneck. In the early years of Rhode Island, wampum was commonly used in trade between the colonists and the Indians, and also in deals among the colonists.

With William Coddington, John Clarke, and a few others, Anne Hutchinson founded a town at the north end of Aquidneck Island. At first they called their town Pocasset (an Indian word), but the name was soon changed to Portsmouth (probably for Portsmouth, England) by Anne Hutchinson and her followers. In spring of 1644 the name of Aquidneck Island was changed to the Island of Rhode Island.

One interesting aspect of early New England colonization was the way splinter groups kept founding new towns. The Pilgrim founders of the Plymouth Colony and the Puritan founders of the Massachusetts Bay Colony had splintered off from the Church of England, although the Puritans had not broken with the Church completely. Roger Williams and Anne Hutchinson had broken off from the Massachusetts Puritans and founded the first two towns in Rhode Island. In 1639 a small group broke away from Anne Hutchinson and her followers and founded Newport, the third Rhode Island town.

William Coddington

Newport's chief founders were William Coddington and John Clarke, who had been Anne Hutchinson's friends but who had argued with her about Portsmouth's government. Coddington, Clarke, and their followers did not go far from Portsmouth. They simply moved to the southern end of the island and founded a town that they named after the town of Newport, England. Just as in England, Portsmouth, Rhode Island is a few miles northeast of Newport.

The fourth town in Rhode Island was founded in 1643 by a group led by Samuel Gorton, one of the most fascinating people in colonial history. Gorton had left England and come to Boston in 1637 in search of what he called "libertie of conscience." Gorton soon became known as a very odd character. He was the founder of a religious

John Clarke

group called the Gortonites who believed that there was no heaven or hell. He signed himself "Professor of the Mysteries of Christ," went into the woods alone in the middle of the night to think, and was said to spend hours each day weeping over all the cruelty in the world. He also fought slavery and the persecution of so-called "witches," and defended people who were abused because of their religious beliefs.

Not finding religious freedom in Boston, Gorton soon moved to the nearby Plymouth Colony, also in present-day Massachusetts. There he got into trouble for defending a woman who was accused of smiling in church. The woman, a maidservant of his wife, was ordered to appear in court. Gorton, who enjoyed arguing with public officials, told her not to appear in court and then presented her case himself. Apparently Gorton insulted the court, for he was fined and ordered to leave Plymouth. Late in 1638, he and his family went to the new town of Portsmouth, Rhode Island.

Samuel Gorton experienced problems in Portsmouth, too. In one incident a cow trespassed onto Gorton's property, and the elderly woman who owned it got into a hair-pulling scuffle with a

In 1641 Samuel Gorton was banished from the Massachusetts Colony.

Gorton's maidservant. The maidservant was called to court; but, just as he had done in Plymouth, Gorton told her not to appear and represented her himself.

Gorton argued bitterly with the Portsmouth judges, and even made a pun about them, saying they were not "justices" but "just asses." It is scary to think of what would have been done to Gorton in Massachusetts for a comment like that! In Portsmouth, Rhode Island, they whipped Gorton in public, jailed him for a while, and then banished him.

Gorton went to Providence, the freethinkers' haven. After living there only a brief time, he began criticizing the Providence government and was asked to leave. He then moved to Pawtuxet, a settlement under the jurisdiction of Providence but outside the town.

Soon the troublemaking Gorton was arguing with the Pawtuxet leaders over religious and political matters. Lacking the strength to get rid of Gorton and his followers, the Pawtuxet colonists asked the Massachusetts Bay Colony for help. The Massachusetts leaders were glad for the chance to help decide matters in Rhode Island, because Massachusetts wanted to take control of the neighboring colony.

Before Massachusetts officials could do anything about Gorton, he and his followers left Pawtuxet. In January 1643 they bought some land from the Narragansett Chief Miantonomo for a large amount of wampum. They built a town, which they at first called Shawomet, on this land. Nothing seemed to go smoothly for Samuel Gorton, however. Two lesser chiefs under Miantonomo complained to Massachusetts authorities that the sale of Shawomet was illegal because they had not received their fair share of the wampum. Massachusetts used this as an excuse once again to try to exert control over Rhode Island.

Authorities in Boston ordered Gorton and several others to come answer the Indians' accusation. Gorton and his followers refused and wrote letters to the Massachusetts officials calling them unfair. For making the faulty sale with the Indians, Gorton probably would have been whipped and jailed for a while. But the Massachusetts authorities claimed they found many cases of "blasphemy" (insulting God) in Gorton's letters. Blasphemy was an offense that could be punished by death in Massachusetts. Although Gorton was living outside their jurdisdiction, in fall of 1643 Massachusetts officials sent about forty soldiers to seize him. After a short battle, Gorton and several Gortonites were taken as prisoners to Boston.

At Gorton's trial, the Indians' complaints were ignored and the "Firebrand of New England" was tried for blasphemy. Gorton was ordered to answer some questions on religious matters. As they knew would happen, the Massachusetts judges did not like Gorton's answers. He was found guilty of blasphemy and came very close to

In 1646 Gorton wrote this book defending his religious beliefs.

Soldiers arrested Gorton and
his followers.

receiving the death penalty. Instead, Gorton and
several of his followers were placed in chains,
paraded around Boston as an example for other
"wrong thinkers," and then jailed for the winter of
1643–1644. They were released in spring of 1644
but warned that if they were found in Massachusetts or in lands claimed by Massachusetts again,
they would be executed.

Samuel Gorton and his followers returned to Rhode Island, where they took refuge for a time on the Island of Rhode Island. Gorton was not one to give up easily. In 1644 he went to England seeking permission to return with his followers to their Shawomet settlement. Gorton became friends with the Earl of Warwick, an English lawmaker who took his side in the dispute with Massachusetts. Thanks to the Earl of Warwick's efforts, King Charles I ordered Massachusetts to stop pestering the Shawomet settlers. The grateful Samuel Gorton changed the name of Shawomet to Warwick when he returned to America. Warwick, which had been first settled in 1643, was the fourth permanent English town in Rhode Island following Providence (1636), Portsmouth (1638), and Newport (1639).

During their first few years, the four towns were not united into a single colony. The meddling of Massachusetts in the Gorton affair and other events showed that it was dangerous for the four towns to stand alone. Roger Williams and others thought that by working together the four towns could withstand dangers that none could face alone. In 1643 the towns of Providence, Portsmouth, and Newport sent Roger Williams to England to obtain an official paper called a charter for a united colony. Due partly to the Earl of Warwick's efforts, the English Parliament (lawmaking body) granted the charter in March 1644. In 1647 Providence, Portsmouth, Newport, and Warwick united under this charter. The charter protected the Rhode Island Colony from raids by outsiders, and extended freedom of religion to all its people.

The Rhode Island Colony had a relatively low population in its early years. By 1650 only about a thousand colonists lived in all of present-day Rhode Island. By 1660 Rhode Island's colonial population was only about 1,500, compared to a population of 20,000 in the Massachusetts Bay Colony, 2,000 in the Plymouth Colony, and 8,500 in little Maryland.

Most Rhode Islanders of the 1600s farmed, as was true throughout the Thirteen Colonies during the entire colonial era. A few families owned large farms and grew wealthy by selling their extra farm products to traders in New York and Massachusetts. Most Rhode Islanders lived on small farms and worked hard to raise enough crops and livestock to feed themselves.

Corn was the main crop grown by the farm families, but peas and oats were also popular. Nearly every Rhode Island farmer raised hogs, and there were also many goats (which provided milk and cheese), cattle, sheep, and horses. The horses reproduced so rapidly after the colonists brought the first ones to Rhode Island that many of them ran wild through the countryside.

Because money was so scarce, the colonists used wampum and farm products when dealing with one another. In Rhode Island's early years, people were allowed to pay taxes with such farm goods as pork (meat from hogs), butter, corn, peas, and oats.

Rhode Island may not have had as many people as most other colonies, but it had a greater variety, especially when it came to religion. In 1657 a number of Quakers (officially called the Religious Society of Friends) came to Rhode Island after being persecuted in Massachusetts and Connecticut. Massachusetts officials advised Rhode Island authorities to expel the Quaker "pests" before the "contagion" (disease) of Quakerism spread throughout New England. Benedict Arnold, the president of Rhode Island and the man who may have built the Old Stone Mill, wrote a noble reply. Rhode Island offered *all* people religious freedom, Arnold wrote, which meant that the Quakers were welcome in the colony. Not only did more Quakers come to Rhode Island after that, settling especially in Newport, but some Rhode Islanders liked the Quaker beliefs so much they joined the Society.

About the time that the first Quakers arrived, another persecuted people came to Rhode Island. These were the Jewish people, who at the time were mistreated nearly everywhere they went in the world. The first group of Jews, consisting of about fifteen families, came to Newport from Europe, and immediately formed the colony's first Jewish congregation.

Early Rhode Island was also home to Puritans, Congregationalists, Church of Englanders, and Baptists. Roger Williams helped found America's first Baptist congregation in Providence in the late 1630s. Besides these well-known groups, there were people like Samuel Gorton who led their own small sects.

Many place names in Rhode Island remind us that the colony was founded as a place where love, justice, and kindness could flourish. There are three islands in Narragansett Bay named Hope, Prudence, and Patience. The state has towns called Hope, Harmony, and Liberty. Providence has streets named Peace, Hope, Benevolent, Benefit, Friendship, and Faith. And in 1647 the colony chose as its motto the single word HOPE, which is still Rhode Island's motto today.

Some colonial Rhode Islanders even expressed the ideas that were dear to them when naming their children. When their first son was born to Roger and Mary Williams in 1638, they christened him Providence. Later they had a daughter named Mercy who married a Warwick, Rhode Island, man called Resolved Waterman. William Harris, one of the small group that helped Roger Williams found Providence, named a son Toleration. There were also children in Rhode Island with such first names as Pardon, Welcome, and Patience.

Outsiders tended to scoff at Rhode Island's ideas. Bostonians called Rhode Island "Rogue Island." A Connecticut minister labeled Rhode Island "a chaos of all Religions" and the "sink" where the other colonies dumped their religious misfits.

Others called Rhode Island much worse than a "sink!" People in New York referred to the colony as the "latrina of New England." *Latrina* is Latin for latrine. Rhode Island was also called "the Island of Error" and the home to "all sorts of riff-raff." The people who made these comments would probably be shocked to know that many of Rhode Island's liberal ideas were later adopted throughout the United States.

ANNE MARBURY HUTCHINSON (1591–1643)

Born in the town of Alford in eastern England, Anne Marbury was the daughter of an outspoken Church of England schoolmaster and preacher. Near the time of Anne's birth, her father, who already had been jailed several times for opposing the Church of England, spoke out again. This time he was fired from his teaching and preaching jobs in Alford and prevented from returning to work for several years.

In 1612 Anne married William Hutchinson, a merchant and sheep farmer from Alford with whom she was to have fifteen children. The year Anne and William were married, the brilliant young minister John Cotton went to work at a church in Boston, England, just twenty-five miles southwest of Alford. Anne and William Hutchinson often traveled the twenty-five miles to hear Reverend Cotton promote Puritan ideas. Anne began holding meetings in her home where she and other people—mostly women—discussed Cotton's sermons and other religious topics.

In 1633, to escape persecution for opposing Church of England beliefs, Reverend Cotton sailed to Boston, Massachusetts, which the Puritans had named for Boston, England. Anne and William Hutchinson decided that their family would also have a better and freer life in the New World. In summer of 1634 the Hutchinson family sailed on the *Griffin* to Boston, where Anne soon became one of the best-liked women in town.

She cared for other women when they were sick and helped them deliver their babies. She also led weekly religious meetings at her house, which were attended by up to 200 women and men. Bostonians walked around town quoting Anne; a number of women became her devoted followers; and small children were heard to ask each other if their parents believed in Anne's ideas.

Just as the Puritans disagreed with the Church of England on some points, Anne Hutchinson had differences with the Puritans. She preached that faith alone was enough to please God, while the Puritans taught that good deeds were also necessary. Anne criticized a prominent minister and sometimes walked out of the church when he spoke. In addition, she claimed that only two Boston ministers were truly godly—John Cotton and John Wheelwright, Anne's outspoken brother-in-law who came to Massachusetts in 1636.

A struggle broke out in Massachusetts over Anne Hutchinson's ideas. At first she had most people's support, but gradually the colony's leaders turned against her, especially after one of her opponents became governor. Even John Cotton abandoned her. In November of 1637 Anne

Hutchinson was placed on trial for "traducing [criticizing] the ministers" of Boston. Her only chance was to beg forgiveness, but Anne would not renounce her ideas. In fact, she criticized her judges, which made things worse for her. She was sentenced to be "banished . . . as being a woman not fit for our society." Until she left, she was to be imprisoned in private homes in the Boston area.

During Anne's imprisonment, William went into the wilderness to find a new home for the family. He and several other Massachusetts exiles bought land from the Indians on Aquidneck Island (now the Island of Rhode Island). In spring of 1638 Anne and her children made the sixty-five-mile trip from Boston to Aquidneck Island by foot and canoe. After traveling for a week, they were reunited with William, who had built a simple cabin. The town Anne helped found on the island was soon named Portsmouth and was the second English town in Rhode Island.

William and Anne Hutchinson loved each other deeply. Massachusetts officials once sent a message to William in Portsmouth asking him to renounce Anne's ideas. William refused, answering that "I am more nearly tied to my wife than to the church, and I look upon her as a dear saint and servant of God."

William Hutchinson died in 1642. Afraid that Rhode Island might soon become part of Massachusetts, Anne Hutchinson then moved to the region of present-day New York City. In 1643, the governor of New York ordered the slaughter of dozens of peaceful Indians in the area. For revenge, the Indians murdered a number of innocent farm people, including Anne Hutchinson and five of her children.

Engraving showing "The Conflict over Weston's Cattle" is an example of the type of argument that frequently broke out between the colonists.

Chapter V

The Growing Colony: Mid-1600s to 1700

Little remains of my ancestors' domain. I am resolved not to see the day when I have no country.

    King Philip

Rhode Island was built by people who had hoped to create a haven for love, justice, and kindness. But by 1660 there was as much friction in Rhode Island as existed in any of the colonies. Rhode Island's small size helped make the arguments even more bitter. There were only a few hundred families in the colony in the mid-1600s, and the towns were just a few miles apart from each other. Everyone knew or knew about nearly everyone else in the colony. There was no escaping from one's rivals by blending in with a large population or by moving far away, unless a person left the colony altogether. To add to the conflict, for many years the same handful of men kept vying with each other for power.

Some of the battles for power sound like melodrama when described today, but they were

King Charles II

very serious to the people involved. For example, at one point William Coddington (one of the founders of Portsmouth and then Newport) sailed off to London, where he obtained a charter naming him lifetime governor of both the Island of Rhode Island and Conanicut Island. This meant that the colony had been split in two—Coddington's islands and the rest of the state. Roger Williams had to go to England, too, where he arranged for the islands to rejoin the rest of the colony and for Coddington's appointment as lifetime governor to be revoked.

There were also many quarrels over land. A number of colonists greedily gobbled up the Indians' lands, incurring the hatred of the Native Americans and of some of their fellow colonists in the process. Furthermore, there were bitter disputes between people over whether portions of Rhode Island should become part of Massachusetts and Connecticut.

Meanwhile, in 1660 there was a major political change in England. During the decade between 1649 and 1659, England had been ruled by a parliament and not by a king or queen, due to the overthrow of King Charles I. In 1660 the monarchy was restored as Charles II became king.

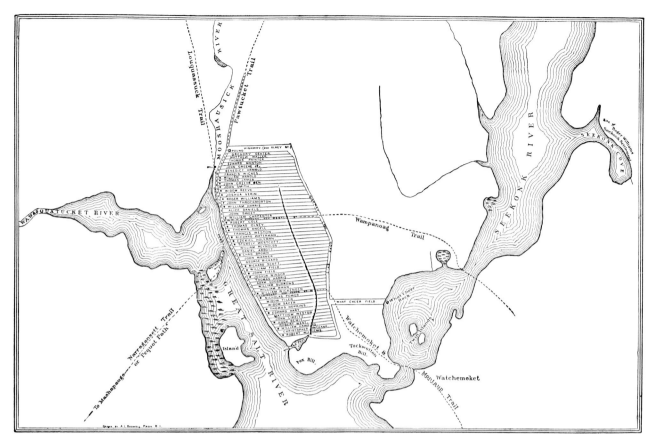

1664 map of Providence shows the lots granted to the settlers and the
Indian trails that served as the only roads through the Rhode Island wilderness.

Rhode Islanders asked Charles II to grant a new
charter continuing their basic rights.

In 1663 the king issued a paper that is often
called the most liberal charter granted by an
English monarch in the colonial age. Besides
guaranteeing complete religious freedom, it
allowed what was called the Colony of Rhode
Island and Providence Plantations a great deal of
self-government. The freemen (male property
owners) were to vote for the colony's lawmakers.

In addition to a governor, deputy governor, and ten assistants, Rhode Island was to have a General Assembly consisting of representatives chosen from the various towns. The Assembly was to make laws, found courts, monitor trade with the Indians, and form emergency troops called militia to protect the colony from attack.

The Charter of 1663 was so respected that it remained the law of Rhode Island for 180 years, well beyond the end of colonial times.* It was replaced by the State Constitution that went into effect in 1843 and is still in effect today.

Throughout colonial America, the Indians watched with growing anger as the colonists set up governments and acted as though the land were all theirs. Gradually the colonists *were* taking over all of the Indians' land. They had many legal and illegal ways to get the land from the Native Americans. Sometimes they flattered the chiefs with presents, then convinced them to sign away their people's lands. If the chiefs did not want to sell, the colonists might loosen them up by giving them what the Indians called "strong water" (liquor). Another trick involved buying land from Indians who were not the real owners. Such Indians were often happy to be paid for land that was not theirs anyway.

* For more information see page 146

The colonists tried to have their own way over the Indians in more than just land purchases. They expected the Indians to obey the white people's laws and do things the white people's way. If a colonist and an Indian had a dispute, the colonists tried to settle the problem in a colonial court. During such trials, the judges almost always took a colonist's word over an Indian's. The only Native Americans who were trusted by many colonists were the Christianized ones known as "praying Indians."

The Wampanoag Chief Massasoit, as he had promised in 1621, kept the peace with the Pilgrims of the Plymouth Colony for the rest of his life, until 1661. Massasoit was succeeded by his oldest son, Wamsutta, whom the colonists called Alexander. In 1662, Plymouth Colony officials ordered Alexander to come prove that his intentions toward them were peaceful. When Alexander refused to appear, the colonists sent armed soldiers to seize him at his hunting lodge in present-day southeastern Massachusetts.

Alexander was sick with a fever by the time he was brought before the Plymouth Colony officials. After he was treated by a doctor, Alexander was allowed to return home, but on the way his condition worsened. The new chief died beneath

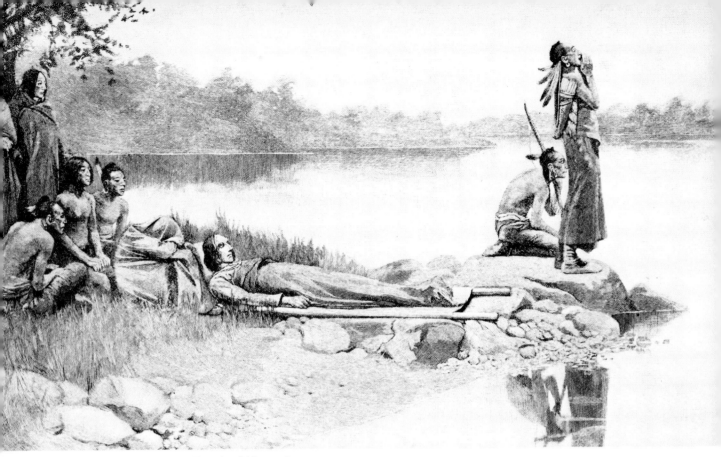

Death of Alexander

an oak tree as his wife, Weetamoe, cradled his
head in her lap.

Weetamoe felt that the colonists had contributed to Alexander's death by forcing him to
come to them and that perhaps the doctor had
even poisoned him. Alexander's younger brother,
Metacomet, who succeeded him as chief, agreed
with Weetamoe. Only about 23 years old when he
became the Wampanoag chief, Metacomet was
known to the colonists as King Philip—the name
most historians use for him.

Already angry at the colonists for taking his people's land, King Philip grew even more bitter after the death of his brother. Plymouth Colony officials realized that Philip was plotting against them from his home at Mount Hope (in present-day Bristol), Rhode Island, and so they arrested him several times. Following an arrest in 1671, Philip and his followers were forced to hand over their firearms, which were then distributed among the English colonists.

King Philip

"My father gave them what they asked," Philip angrily said about this. "They have had townships and whole Indian kingdoms for a few blankets, hoes, and flattering words. But they are not content—the white man's throat is wide."

One reason the Indians usually lost their battles with the colonists was that different tribes rarely banded together as allies. Part of Philip's greatness as a leader was his ability to coax warriors of various tribes to fight on the same side. He convinced many Narragansetts, Nipmucs, Pocassets, and Sakonnets to help him drive the colonists out of New England. The conflict in which Philip tried to do this is known as *King Philip's War*. It began in late June 1675 when the Indians killed a number of colonists at Swansea,

Massachusetts, just across from eastern Rhode Island.

There are many stories about the cruelty of both sides during King Philip's War. Most of Philip's attacks were aimed at Massachusetts towns, which he burned down by shooting flaming arrows at the wooden houses. The Indians scalped and tortured some of their victims, but the colonists were guilty of just as many horrors. For example, at Natick, Massachusetts the colonists massacred over 120 Indians; and at the Massachusetts town of Springfield they ordered an old Indian woman torn apart by dogs.

Rhode Island was not nearly as hard hit as Massachusetts by King Philip's War. But it was the site of two key events in the war: the Great Swamp Fight and the death of King Philip.

In late 1675 the colonists learned that thousands of Philip's followers were spending the winter at the Narragansett Indian village in the Great Swamp, near what is now Kingston, Rhode Island. The village, located on an island in the swamp, consisted of about five hundred wigwams and three thousand people. For protection, the

Indians had surrounded the village with a high wooden fence made of pointed stakes.

A New England army consisting of about a thousand men set out to destroy this village. The colonial soldiers were led by Plymouth Colony Governor Josiah Winslow, who was aided by Captain Benjamin Church, an experienced Indian fighter from Rhode Island. However, Rhode Islanders for the most part refused to have anything to do with the war. Only a few of them had joined this army, which consisted mostly of men from Massachusetts Bay, Plymouth, and Connecticut.

The colonial forces approached the Great Swamp through a heavy snowstorm on the afternoon of December 19, 1675. At two in the afternoon, the colonists attacked. At first the Indians guarding the village held back the enemy. Finally, Benjamin Church and thirty men broke through the fortifications. After a fierce battle the Indians began to flee, and the soldiers poured into the village.

The colonial army then perpetrated one of the biggest massacres of Indians in American history. Captain Church tried to stop them from doing so,

Colonial army attacking an Indian village

but the soldiers set the Indian village on fire. As had happened at the burning of the Pequots' village in Connecticut in 1637, hundreds of Indians were burned to death. Hundreds more were slain as they fled, their blood turning the snow around the village red. In all, about a thousand Indian men, women, and children were killed in this Great Swamp Fight, while the colonists lost about two hundred men.

Philip, who had been in the New York region at the time of the massacre, continued to direct attacks against the colonists. In February and March of 1676 the Indians attacked many Massachusetts and several Rhode Island settlements. Then in late March the Indians prepared to attack the town of Providence.

By this time Roger Williams' two old Indian friends, the Narragansett chiefs Canonicus and Miantonomo, were dead. Canonicus had died in 1647 at about the age of 80. Miantonomo had been captured by the Mohegans during a battle in 1643, and had been sent to Boston officials who wanted to destroy the Narragansetts' power. Not wanting his blood on their own hands, the Boston authorities had arranged for an enemy chief to execute Miantonomo. By 1676, Canonchet, the son of the executed Miantonomo, was the Narragansett chief.

Providence officials had learned of the coming attack, and by the time Canonchet approached with his warriors, only several dozen of the town's one thousand people remained. Among them was Roger Williams, who was about 73 years old and lame, partly due to his difficult trip through the wilderness when coming to Rhode Island many years earlier. Williams limped out to meet Chief Canonchet, who was thought to be only in his

The Indians attacked the settlers, too.

early twenties. It was said that Williams spent an hour trying to convince Canonchet to spare the town. Finally Williams warned the young chief that the king of England would keep sending soldiers until the Indians were beaten. Canonchet was said to have answered: "Well, let them come, we are ready for them. But as for you, Brother Williams, you are a good man. You have been kind to us many years. Not a hair of your head shall be touched."

The Indians did not harm Roger Williams, but they burned about half of the town's approximately eighty houses. They killed one person in Providence, a man named Wright whom they must have especially hated because they cut him open and stuck his Bible inside him.

A few days later a colonial force captured Canonchet in Connecticut. Reportedly the Connecticut forces that had captured him offered Canonchet his life if he promised that his people would surrender. Canonchet refused. When told he was to die, the young Narragansett chief reportedly answered, "I like it well. I shall die before my heart is soft, or I have said anything unworthy of myself." Canonchet was executed in southeastern Connecticut, not far from where the Pequots had been slaughtered thirty-nine years earlier. His captors and executioners sent his head to the Connecticut town of Hartford "as a token of love and affection," as they put it.

Benjamin Church had been wounded at the Great Swamp Fight, but by summer of 1676 he had healed well enough to reenter the war against Philip. Plymouth Governor Josiah Winslow placed Captain Church in charge of a force of about two hundred men—sixty colonists and more than a hundred Indians who were hostile to Philip. Church and his forces tracked Philip to a swamp in southeastern Massachusetts, where in July 1676 they killed or captured nearly two hundred Indians. Philip's wife and son were among those captured, but Philip escaped. Church soon learned that Philip had taken refuge at his home at Mount Hope, Rhode Island.

The great Wampanoag chief liked to sleep on a huge rock that is now known as "King Philip's Throne" at Mount Hope. On the night of August 11, 1676, Philip went to sleep on the rock with one of his lieutenants, Anawon, lying nearby. It was said that on that last night Philip awakened from a nightmare and told Anawon that he had dreamed of being captured by Church.

As the sun rose on the morning of August 12, Benjamin Church and his men approached Philip and his remaining warriors. There was no escaping this ambush for Philip. He was shot to death by an Indian who was fighting on the colonial side.

Although fighting continued in Maine and New Hampshire for about two more years, the war in southern New England (present-day Massachusetts, Connecticut, and Rhode Island) ended soon after Philip's death. King Philip's War had been very costly to both sides. About a thousand colonists had been killed, and about half of New England's nearly one hundred settlements had been attacked, with about a dozen of them suffering total destruction.

The Indians had suffered much more. Several thousands of them had been killed, and several hundred more, including Philip's wife and son, were sold into slavery. Two major tribes, the Wampanoags and the Narragansetts, had been nearly wiped out. As a final grisly note to the end of a grisly war, Benjamin Church's men cut off Philip's head and sent it as a trophy to Plymouth, where it was displayed on a pole until around the year 1700.

For the colonists in Rhode Island and the rest of New England,* the end to King Philip's War meant they could build towns and farms on land that had once belonged to the Indians. Between 1676

King Philip was killed.

* For more information about New England's government see page 147

and the year 1700, Rhode Island's colonial population more than doubled, rising from about 2,500 to about 6,000. New towns were settled during those years. Besides the four original towns of Providence, Portsmouth, Newport, and Warwick, by 1700 settlements had also been founded at what are now Pawtucket, Bristol, East Greenwich, Kingston, Westerly, Woonsocket, and Cranston.

KING PHILIP (METACOMET) (1639?–1676)

Massasoit, chief of the Wampanoags of southeastern Massachusetts and eastern Rhode Island, was a great friend to the English colonists. He attended the Pilgrims' first Thanksgiving in fall of 1621, and also sheltered Roger Williams after he was expelled from Massachusetts. After Massasoit's death, his oldest son, called Alexander by the English, ruled briefly. Upon Alexander's death in 1662, Metacomet, who was called King Philip by the English, became chief.

Philip's personality was a fascinating blend of toughness, loyalty, and tenderness. As a youth, he had passed the Wampanoags' test of manhood by spending the winter alone in the forest with only his hatchet, bow and arrow, and knife for protection. He was so strong that his people claimed he could throw a stone two miles through the air from his home at Mount Hope, Rhode Island. He was so loyal that he once rowed forty miles while chasing an Indian who had made a comment about the dead Massasoit. Loyalty to his dead brother, Alexander, was one reason why King Philip began fighting the New England colonists in 1675. Philip also knew that the colonists would take all of the Indians' land unless someone stopped them.

The colonial leaders portrayed Philip as a bloodthirsty villain, because that made it easier for them to recruit soldiers to fight him. But the truth was that Philip hated the war almost as much as he hated the colonists. While giving the command for the war to begin, Philip reportedly fell to the ground crying because of all the bloodshed that he knew would follow. He also felt sorry for his enemies, as demonstrated by this remarkable note from him to Plymouth officials:

> *You know and we know your heart great sorrowful with crying for your lost many many hundred men and all your house and all your land and woman, child and cattle as all your thing that you have lost....*

Philip and his people had no chance to win King Philip's War, because the colonists had more soldiers and better weapons. By mid-1676, many of Philip's friends and relatives had been killed, his wife and son had been captured, and many others had deserted him and joined the English side. An Indian working for the colonists shot Philip to death at Mount Hope in summer of 1676. For many years New England colonists told stories about how their ancestors had fought the wicked King Philip, but it should be remembered that Philip had fought to save his people's land.

Harbor and city of Newport, Rhode Island about 1730

Chapter VI

Planters, Pirates, Slaves, and Ships: 1700–1756

Rhode Island is a place where pirates are ordinarily too kindly entertained.

> *Spoken at a trial of a pirate in London*

To be Sold by John Banister at his House in Newport . . . a fine Parcel of Negro Men, Women, Boys and Girls, imported directly from the Gold Coast, and they are esteemed to be the finest Cargo of Slaves ever brought into New England.

> *Notice of a sale of slaves posted in Newport in 1752*

Most of the 6,000 colonists who lived in Rhode Island in the early 1700s owned small- or medium-sized farms. A few owned very large farms which resembled the large plantations of the southern colonies. The aristocratic families who lived in big homes on large tracts of land near the western shores of Narragansett Bay were sometimes called "Narragansett Planters." Black slaves raised the sheep and cattle and produced the butter and cheese which contributed to the Planters' wealth.

Agriculture was the most popular way of life, but by the early 1700s many Rhode Islanders earned their livings from the sea rather than from the farm. Newport, Providence, and other coastal towns were shipbuilding centers by that time. Merchants who lived in the coastal towns sent these ships out to ports in other colonies and also to foreign ports in distant lands. Among the products bought and sold by Rhode Island merchants were beef, sugar, rum, wool, fancy cloth, silk stockings, glassware, tools, weapons, and people.

Unfortunately, listing "people" with the other products is not a mistake. A number of Rhode Island merchants bought and sold black slaves. During the early 1700s slavery was legal in all the colonies, and there were several hundred black slaves in Rhode Island by that time. However, relatively few of the slaves that were shipped to Rhode Island remained to work in the colony. Most of them stayed only briefly before being sold to people in other colonies.

During colonial times about a fifth of all the slaves shipped to America made the voyage in ships owned by Rhode Islanders. Newport, Bristol, and Providence were important centers for selling

TO BE SOLD, by
JOHN LYON,
At *REHOBOTH:*
TWENTY-THREE fine healthy young Slaves, juſt arrived from the Coaſt of Africa.—For Directions and further Information, apply to WILLIAM PROUD, in *Providence.*

Advertisement from the *Providence Gazette and Country Journal,* June 11, 1763

Slaves were captured in Africa and shipped to North America.

slaves; and Rhode Island as a whole was one of the main slave-trading centers in all the world.

The people who earned fortunes selling slaves called it a business, but to the slaves the system was a terrible tragedy. The process began when African chiefs chained people they planned to sell and marched them to the coast. Generally these people were war prisoners or had angered the rulers in some way. Upon reaching the coast, the slaves were locked in a stockade. When a slave-trading ship reached the African coast, the captain bought the slaves, then packed them below deck for the trip to America.

During the voyage, which usually took several months, each slave was chained inside a space smaller than a coffin. Commonly a number of slaves died before their ship reached its destination, which could be Rhode Island, another East Coast port, or an island in the Caribbean Sea. The slaves who made it safely were sold for large sums of money, making the people in the slave business very rich.

Captain Kidd

Some Rhode Island sea captains and ship-owners were involved in piracy as well as slave trading. Many people have romantic notions about pirates, but in truth they were robbers who worked at sea. Instead of opposing pirates, Rhode Island had a reputation for welcoming them. For example, the famed William Kidd, a sea captain who was thought to have turned pirate, spent much time in Rhode Island and was said to have been backed by a number of Rhode Island merchants. A legend was told that Captain Kidd hid some treasure on Conanicut Island in Narragansett Bay, but there is no evidence that any of it has been discovered. Rhode Island officials generally let the pirates alone. Samuel Cranston, who served as Rhode Island governor from 1698 to his death in 1727, was accused of befriending pirates.

Romantic pirate painting entitled "Capture of the Galleon"

There were reasons why several colonies including Rhode Island and New York became pirate havens. Nearly everyone gained from piracy. Because pirates sold their stolen goods rather cheaply, people could save money by buying from them. Shopkeepers and tavern owners usually liked having pirates around because they spent money freely. Today it is wrong for lawmakers to take bribes (payoffs) in exchange for ignoring illegal activities. But in colonial times, lawmakers were widely expected to take bribes, and many did so rather openly. Pirates often paid lawmakers large bribes to let them alone, which made the lawmakers happy. The main losers from piracy were the shipowners whose goods were stolen. In many cases, however, the owners lived far away and could do little about it.

Nevertheless, criticism from English officials finally prompted Governor Cranston to act against the pirates. On July 19, 1723, twenty-six pirates were hanged at Newport, Rhode Island. Although piracy still occurred off Rhode Island's coast and pirates still landed on its shores, after this event the heyday of piracy was over for the little colony.

Thousands of men called *privateers* also sailed out of Rhode Island ports. People tend to confuse privateers with pirates. While pirates were sea robbers who worked for themselves, privateers were private citizens hired by the government to attack enemy ships. The ships in which the privateers sailed were also called *privateers*.

The privateering ships and sailors were valuable to the English government. Between the mid-1600s and the mid-1700s Britain fought a series of wars with France, The Netherlands, and Spain. Britain did not have enough vessels to attack so many enemy ships, so English officials hired privateers to help them. When enemy cargo was seized by the privateers, it was sold. Then much of this money was distributed among the owners, officers, and crew of the privateer.

One reason people confuse privateers with pirates was that privateers often became pirates. The privateer sailors were a hardy bunch, willing to risk death in sea battles for a chance to share in a rich prize. Things were fine as long as the privateers were able to find and overcome enemy ships. When weeks passed with no sign of the enemy, privateers often turned to piracy. The famous Captain Kidd started as a privateer, but later was accused of having turned pirate.

Rhode Island was the leading colony for privateering in the colonial era. Several thousand Rhode Islanders sailed out of the colony's ports on hundreds of privateering ships throughout those years. During King George's War alone, which

Britain fought against France between 1744 and 1748, Rhode Island privateers reportedly seized over a hundred French ships. Some Rhode Island shipowners became extremely wealthy from the gold, silks, ivory, and other goods that their privateering ships brought back. They built huge mansions with their profits.

Whale hunting became another way that Rhode Islanders made money from the sea. During the 1740s a Spanish Jew named Jacob Rodrigues Rivera moved to Newport. Rivera soon introduced a way of making candles from the spermaceti (waxy substance) in the heads of sperm whales. This helped promote both the whaling and the candle-making industries in Rhode Island. Providence, Warren, Bristol, and Newport sent out whaling ships, and soon there were more than a dozen candle-making shops in Newport alone.

The first half of the eighteenth century was also a time when things worked out well for Rhode Island in its border disputes. For many years, Connecticut had sought much of what is now western Rhode Island. During the late 1720s British officials agreed on a western boundary for

Carved wooden figurehead from a whaling ship

Rhode Island that denied Connecticut the land it sought. During the 1740s British officials granted Rhode Island the eastern towns of Cumberland, Warren, Bristol, Tiverton, and Little Compton, which had been claimed by Massachusetts.

This southwest view of Newport was engraved about 1795.

Chapter VII

Life in Rhode Island in the 1750s

A true Rhode Islander would not dream of using an "h" in jonnycake.

Imogene Wolcott, The Yankee Cook Book

One big difference between Rhode Island in the 1750s and the modern state is the change in population. As of 1980, the Ocean State was home to almost a million people. Back in the 1750s, the population of all Thirteen Colonies added together was not much above a million! Of that number, about 40,000 lived in Rhode Island—roughly 1/25th the population the state has today.

Not only were Rhode Island's towns much smaller back in the 1750s, their rank in size was different. As of 1980, Rhode Island's largest cities were Providence, Warwick, Cranston, Pawtucket, East Providence, Woonsocket, and Newport in that order. As the chart shows, in 1755 Newport was by far the colony's largest town, with Providence a distant second:

RHODE ISLAND POPULATIONS

Six Biggest Towns in 1755	Population in 1755	Population in 1980 (rank in size)
1. Newport	6,800	29,000 (#3)
2. Providence	3,200	157,000 (#1)
3. Westerly	2,300	14,000 (#6)
4. North Kingston	2,100	22,000 (#4)
5. Warwick	1,900	87,000 (#2)
6. Smithfield	1,900	17,000 (#5)

Newport was Rhode Island's commercial center as well as its population leader. The sea was very important to Newport. Hundreds of Newport men worked as sailors and many others were shipbuilders.

Thanks largely to the money brought in by shipping, Newport reached its peak of prosperity in the mid-1700s. A few of the city's merchants and shipowners grew quite wealthy. They built mansions for themselves as well as lovely public buildings during those years. The Old Colony House, where Rhode Island lawmakers met, went up in 1739. By 1750 it had a reputation as one of the two or three most attractive public buildings in the Thirteen Colonies. In 1744, at a cost of

$100,000 (which would equal millions of dollars today) the merchant Godfrey Malbone built the first of the huge Newport homes. In 1750 work was completed on the Redwood Library (today Rhode Island's oldest library), which the merchant Abraham Redwood helped finance.*

Of the rich Newport merchants, Godfrey Malbone became particularly famous for his glamorous life-style. Malbone held great feasts at his home for his returning ship captains. Just for sport, Malbone allowed the captains to smash all the dishes and glasses on the table at the end of each feast. He did not extend that privilege to his other guests. In 1756 George Washington of Virginia celebrated his twenty-fourth birthday at the Malbone house. When the young Virginian dropped a punch bowl, he had to pay four pounds (about ten dollars) for it right then and there!

During one dinner party, a fire broke out in an upper story of the Malbone house. Soon it became apparent that his servants could not put out the flames. Malbone was so rich that the loss of his mansion did not seem to upset him. "If I have lost my house, I shall not lose my dinner!" he said. He and his wife had their servants place the tables outside on the lawn, where the party continued by the light of the burning house.

* For more information about money in Rhode Island see page 148

Another time, after being thanked for giving money to some cause, Godfrey Malbone said, "What will not money buy?" This comment was passed around Newport, and the next day this little rhyme was found posted at the Town Hall: "All the money in the place, won't buy old Malbone a handsome face." Malbone offered a reward to learn the identity of the poet, and good-naturedly paid it when the culprit admitted the deed.

There are many amusing stories about Godfrey Malbone and Newport's other rich merchants. It must be remembered, however, that many of the merchants had become wealthy by buying and selling slaves. By 1750, dozens of Newport ships, including ones belonging to Godfrey Malbone and Abraham Redwood, were regularly sailing to Africa, where their captains exchanged rum and other goods for slaves. Although some of the slaves were sold in Rhode Island, many others were sold to islands in the Caribbean Sea.

Some merchants who engaged in slave trading knew it was wrong, but they couldn't resist the large profits it brought them. A number of records regarding slave trading in Rhode Island still exist. For example, a ship called the *Elizabeth* set sail from Africa with seventy black slaves aboard, but by the time the vessel reached Rhode Island in early 1754 eight of the slaves had died. Records show that the remaining nineteen women, fifteen men, seventeen boys, and eleven girls brought in a total of nearly 2,000 pounds in English money, which would be worth tens of thousands of dollars today.

The old records also tell heartbreaking stories of entire shiploads of slaves going down at sea. If a slave ship sank in a storm, the sailors often were able to save themselves, but the slaves chained below the decks were usually abandoned. During the mid-1700s, a number of shiploads of slaves belonging to Godfrey Malbone and other merchants sank off the African coast.

Newport people were accustomed to the deaths of their own men at sea, too. In 1750 many Newport families were still grieving over a terrible disaster that had occurred five years earlier. Two big ships belonging to Godfrey Malbone had set off in a blizzard on the day before Christmas of 1745. Both ships had been lost, resulting in the deaths of nearly all the sailors.

Until 1758, Rhode Islanders who wanted to learn about events at sea and other news had to rely on word of mouth or obtain newspapers from other colonies. Rhode Island had briefly had a newspaper back in 1732–1733, when James Franklin (brother of the famous Ben Franklin) had published the *Rhode Island Gazette.* But the *Gazette* had failed after only about eight months. In 1758 James Franklin's son, who was also named James, began the colony's second paper, the *Newport Mercury.* Not counting a brief time during the Revolutionary War, the *Newport Mercury* has been coming out continuously for more than two centuries.

One reason why the *Gazette* had failed was that few Rhode Islanders could read, compared to the percentages in other colonies. Rhode Island had the worst educational system in all of New England. Back in 1647 the Massachusetts Bay Colony had passed a law requiring each Massachusetts town of fifty or more families to have a school that was partly paid for by taxes. This had been the start of America's public-school system. Every New England colony except Rhode Island adopted the Massachusetts public-school system. Rhode Island lacked a system of public education until well after the end of the colonial era.

Many wealthy young people in Newport and the other towns received a fine education despite the lack of public schools. Religious groups operated

New England schoolhouse

some schools, while a few private schools were run by schoolmasters and schoolmistresses. Wealthy families often hired tutors, many of whom were from England, to teach Latin, Greek, and other subjects to their sons. No girls went to college, but a handful of boys went on to Harvard in Massachusetts and Yale in Connecticut. Rhode Island did not have its own college until 1764, when Rhode Island College (later named Brown University) was founded at Warren. In 1770 the school moved to Providence, where Brown University is still located.

In the late 1700s, Providence surpassed Newport in population. But during the 1750s Providence was still the colony's number two city. Like Newport, Providence depended a great deal on the sea. It was a shipbuilding and privateering center, and some of its merchants sent out slave ships. Providence's leading merchant family, the four Brown brothers (Nicholas, Joseph, John, and Moses), built schools and churches and helped make other improvements in the town. The Brown brothers helped establish Rhode Island College. The name was later changed to Brown University to honor Nicholas Brown, son of Nicholas, one of the four Brown brothers.

Nicholas Brown

The 1750s were years of great growth in Providence. During that decade Providence built a special shelter called an almshouse for its homeless poor, established a fire department, and created its first library. Also at that time, Providence began taking steps toward creating a public-school system. Although public schools were not established throughout Providence until about the year 1800, that was still thirty years before the founding of public schools throughout the rest of the state.

In the countryside south of Providence, near Narragansett Bay, lived some wealthy farmers

Wealthy planters lived in fine homes.

called Narragansett Planters. These people often owned slaves and enjoyed a life-style similar to that of the rich Southern planters. However, most Rhode Islanders were neither as rich as the Narragansett Planters and Newport slave merchants, nor as poor as the people in the Providence almshouse. Most Rhode Islanders of the 1750s were farmers who lived rather simply and worked hard to feed and raise their families.*

* For more information about workers see page 149

Rhode Island's farm families produced most of their own food. They grew corn and beans, and raised cows, sheep, and pigs. Those who lived near Narragansett Bay went down near the water's edge with their baskets and gathered clams, shrimp, and lobsters for the family table.

The fathers and older sons did the heavy farm work, while the mothers and older daughters prepared the food. They cooked in big pots that

Most Rhode Island farmers worked the land with their families.

were suspended over the fireplace, and baked in a brick oven near the fireplace. Jonny cakes—a kind of cornmeal bread—were eaten throughout New England, but a variety made in Rhode Island became the best known. Some Rhode Islanders ate Rhode Island jonny cakes three times a day—for breakfast, midday dinner (what we now call lunch), and supper. For variety, cooks sometimes added huckleberries or blueberries to the jonny cake batter.

Various stories were told about how jonny cakes got their name. Rhode Islanders generally believed that they were originally called journey cakes because people took them to eat on long trips. Many New Englanders pronounced the words journey cakes so that they sounded like jonny cakes, and this was why the spelling was changed.

Rhode Island mothers also prepared fish chowders, meat stews, and succotash for their families. In those days, water wasn't a popular drink, because the people didn't know how to purify it. Adults and as children drank tea. They also drank hard cider, beer, and other alcoholic beverages.

Besides the cooking, the mothers did most of the child raising and clothes making. Although

Spinning wheels turned wool into yarn.

some families bought their "Sunday clothes" in town, the typical farm mother made many of her family's everyday clothes. She gathered wool from the family sheep and made it into wool yarn on her spinning wheel. She gathered flax from her garden and spun it into linen yarn. After making the yarn into cloth on her foot-powered loom, she sewed the fabric into petticoats and trousers, aprons and gowns, shirts and blankets.

Children usually awakened very early to tend the livestock, fetch water, and make soap. Few Rhode Island children during the 1750s attended school, but most learned to read and write a bit anyway. As the family sat around the fireplace at night, the parents taught their children to read from their Bible, which was the only book found in many households.

Life wasn't all work for the farm families. Children played the English game of cricket, as well as a football game that resembled modern soccer. Many men liked to go to the taverns in the towns where they sat talking and playing cards with their friends. By the year 1750, Providence alone had thirty taverns. Horseracing was also popular with the men. Among the horses they raced were the famed Narragansett Pacers. Developed in the Narragansett country, the Pacers were smooth-running horses that unfortunately are extinct today.

SHIPPING HORSES wanted.

NICHOLAS BROWN, and COMPANY, Want to buy immediately, a few likely SURINAM HORSES.

Advertisement from the *Providence Gazette,* January 7, 1764.

Like people in the other colonies, the Rhode Island farm families also found ways to make their work fun. Since husking corn could be boring when done alone, friends and neighbors gathered for "cornhusking bees." Women exchanged cloth scraps and then sewed them into beautiful quilts at "quilting bees." One quilting bee in the Narragansett country in 1752 was said to have lasted for ten days.

The British were unable to collect taxes from the Stamp Act.

Chapter VIII

The Revolutionary War Begins

Oh America! What a black cloud hangs over this once happy land, but now miserable and afflicted people.

Nathanael Greene, writing shortly after the start of the Revolutionary War

THE FRENCH AND INDIAN WARS

England had its colonies along the East Coast of what is now the United States, but England's ancient enemy, France, also controlled some American lands. France ruled part of Canada, which it called New Canada, to the north of the Thirteen American Colonies. England and France each wanted the other's North American lands. In addition, both had their eyes on a huge land tract in what is now the middle of the United States.

Over a seventy-four-year period, England and France fought four wars for control of North American territory. These wars are known as the French and Indian Wars, or the Colonial Wars. Individually, the four were King William's War (1689-1697), Queen Anne's War (1702-1713),

King George's War (1744-1748), and the French and Indian War (1754-1763).

On one side were the French, their Indian allies, and some Canadians. Against them were the British, the colonists, and their smaller number of Indian friends. The Indians had reasons to favor the French over the English. The French mainly wanted to trade with the Indians while the English always wanted to take more and more of the Indians' land.

No major fighting took place in Rhode Island during these wars, but the colony was very much involved in the conflicts anyway. Rhode Island men participated in expeditions against the French in Canada, and hundreds of Rhode Island privateers and privateering ships also helped the British cause.

The long struggle over North American lands was finally decided after Britain won the fourth war, the French and Indian War. According to the peace treaty that was made in 1763, Canada passed into British control.

EVENTS LEADING TO THE REVOLUTION

Most of the time between the 1600s and the 1760s the colonists had been content with British rule. The laws known as the Navigation Acts had caused some friction. These laws tried to force the colonists to trade only with England. However, the colonists got around the Navigation Acts by smuggling goods from other countries into American ports. England knew about this smuggling, but did little to stop it. Britain also allowed the colonists a great deal of self-government, especially in Rhode Island, while providing protection for the Americans against the French and the Indians.

Everything changed after Britain won the French and Indian War. The war had been very costly, and the lawmakers in the British Parliament in England were having trouble coming up with the necessary funds. Some members of Parliament argued that since the Americans had gained from the victory over France (they no longer had to worry about French conquest), they should pay some of the bill in the form of taxes. Other British lawmakers, with a better understanding of the Americans, warned that taxing the colonists heavily would make them extremely angry.

The British lawmakers who favored American taxation won out. Starting in 1764, the British tried to make the Americans pay taxes on such items as sugar, tea, paper, paint, and newspapers.

Britain also began working to enforce its Navigation Acts, so that the colonists would not do business with non-British countries.

The Americans *were* extremely angry over these new tax laws, just as some British lawmakers had warned. One tax that especially angered them was the Stamp Act, which was to go into effect on November 1, 1765. Throughout the Thirteen Colonies, Americans protested this law, which required them to buy special stamps and place them on newspapers, wills, marriage licenses, and various other legal papers. The Americans burned dummies that were made to look like British officials. Groups of American patriots called "Sons of Liberty" smashed property owned by British officials.

Tax stamp

The Stamp Act prompted a great deal of protest in Rhode Island. In early June 1765 a mob of Rhode Islanders seized a small boat belonging to the British ship *Maidstone* and burned it in Newport. This was one of the first destructive acts against the British during the Revolutionary era. Rhode Islanders also hanged and then burned a dummy of a British stamp official, and then damaged the man's house.

Afraid that the Americans would become even more violent, Parliament repealed the Stamp Act

To protest the stamp tax, the colonists hung dummies of the tax collectors.

in early 1766. Throughout the Thirteen Colonies, Americans celebrated by firing cannons and ringing church bells. To remind them that Britain was still in charge, Parliament also declared that the Americans had to obey the parent country in the future.

The British kept passing new tax laws, which the Americans kept disobeying. During the late

1760s and early 1770s there were small acts of rebellion throughout the colonies. In 1769 the British sloop *Liberty* seized two ships from Connecticut waters, charging their captains with smuggling. The Connecticut vessels were brought to Newport Harbor. While the *Liberty's* crew was in Newport, a mob that may have been a mixture of Connecticut and Rhode Island Sons of Liberty cut the British ship's cables and then towed the vessel toward Newport. The Americans threw everything of value from the *Liberty* into the water and then burned the vessel. Because of all the defiant acts that were then taking place in the colonies, the British could not track down and punish the guilty parties.

Rhode Island's most famous act of rebellion before the actual start of the Revolutionary War was the burning of the British ship, *Gaspee*, in June 1772. The heavily armed *Gaspee* was assigned to curb smuggling in Narragansett Bay. Its commander, Lieutenant William Dudingston, was hated by Rhode Islanders. To harass them, he searched little boats that were carrying farm goods from town to town, and sometimes even seized legal cargoes.

Newport people protested to a British admiral about Dudingston. Instead of investigating the matter, the admiral threatened to hang any Newporters who tried to stop Dudingston from seizing a ship. A Rhode Island sea captain named Benjamin Lindsey decided to strike back at Dudingston.

Sailing out of Newport, Lindsey brought his schooner, *Hannah*, tauntingly close to the *Gaspee*. Lieutenant Dudingston gave chase, but Captain Lindsey had a plan. His vessel was lighter and faster than Dudingston's, and it was said that he knew every sandbar and inlet of Narragansett Bay. Near Warwick on the west side of Narragansett Bay, Captain Lindsey headed for a sandbar, then quickly changed course to avoid it. Lieutenant Dudingston saw the sandbar, but too late. The *Gaspee* soon ran aground on it. Captain Lindsey sailed into Providence, where he told the American patriot John Brown (one of the four Brown brothers) about the beached *Gaspee*. Brown organized a raiding party.

A group of armed American patriots left a waterfront tavern in Providence at about ten o'clock on the night of June 9, 1772. The Americans towed out to the sandbar where the *Gaspee* was still stuck. A British watchman on the *Gaspee* called "Who comes there?" as the Americans approached. When there was no answer, the watchman went to get Dudingston, who repeated the question.

The leader of the raiders, Captain Abraham Whipple, reportedly was very insulting to Dudingston. "I have got a warrant to apprehend you, goddam you," Whipple was reported to have said, "so surrender, goddam you."

A young American named Joseph Bucklin was said to have borrowed a musket from a young boy standing near him. "I can kill that fellow," Bucklin supposedly said, and then fired the gun just as Captain Whipple finished cursing out Dudingston. The British lieutenant fell with a serious bullet wound to the groin.

Exactly who said what and who fired the shot is not known for certain, but it is a fact that Dudingston was shot. An American who knew a little surgery stopped the bleeding and bandaged the wound. The Americans then forced the British sailors to leave the *Gaspee* and row ashore in their longboats. After setting the *Gaspee* ablaze, the Americans rowed back to Providence, too.

The reason we lack details of the *Gaspee* incident was that the Americans could not brag about the deed. Britain had recently made the burning of one of its ships a crime punishable by death, and on top of that the Americans had shot

Abraham Whipple

Oil painting by Charles DeWolf Brownell, "The Burning of the Gaspee," 1892

a British officer. Hoping to find and punish the raiders as an example to other Americans, the British held an investigation.* Apparently the names of the attackers were known throughout Rhode Island; but because Rhode Islanders would not testify against them, the raiders were not punished.

Despite the *Gaspee* burning in Rhode Island and incidents in other colonies, Massachusetts was the center of American unrest. There was so much protest in Boston that the British sent

* For more information see page 150

soldiers there to keep order. Bostonians hated being watched over by these British soldiers, whom they called "redcoats" and "lobsterbacks" because of their red uniforms. On March 5, 1770, a group of Bostonians hurled stones at some British soldiers. The redcoats fired into the crowd, killing five people. Even though the colonists had started this fight, Samuel Adams of Boston and other American patriots called it the "Boston Massacre."

Nearly four years later, on December 16, 1773, a group of Bostonians who had dressed as Indians to hide their identities boarded three British ships. To show what they thought of the tax on tea, they dumped 340 chests of British tea into Boston Harbor. This became known as the "Boston Tea Party" and was a key event leading up to the Revolutionary War. In June 1774, Britain punished Bostonians for their tea party by closing the port of Boston. This was a hardship for Bostonians, because it meant that vital supplies could not enter their city by ship. However, colonists in neighboring Rhode Island, Connecticut, and New York sent in beef, fish, corn, and sugar, while Carolina colonists sent in rice over land. These supplies helped the people of Boston survive.

All the talk that was going on about people's "rights" got Rhode Islanders thinking about slavery, which totally deprived black people of their rights. In June 1774—the same month that the Boston port was closed—Rhode Island became the first colony to outlaw the importing of slaves. Stephen Hopkins was one of the Rhode Island officials who helped get this law passed.

Meanwhile, the colonists realized that they had to band together if they were to get their way with Britain over taxes and other matters. In fall of 1774 the colonists held a big meeting in Philadelphia, Pennsylvania, to decide how to deal with Britain. Every colony but Georgia attended this meeting, which was called the *First Continental Congress*.

Stephen Hopkins

Rhode Island sent Stephen Hopkins and Samuel Ward to that First Continental Congress, which opened on September 5, 1774. The lawmakers of the Rhode Island Assembly gave Hopkins and Ward these instructions. They were to advise Congress to send a letter of complaint to Britain's King George III, and they were to promote future meetings of colonial representatives.

Although all the members of the First Continental Congress wanted fairer treatment from Britain, most delegates wanted to avoid a war, and few thought that America was ready to separate from the parent country. However, Congress told the colonial governments to get their militias ready in case war came about. Congress also sent letters to Britain outlining the American complaints. Before closing on October 26, 1774, the delegates laid plans for another meeting in the spring if British lawmakers would not change their ways.

In Rhode Island and other colonies, the American patriots took out their guns that in many cases had not been used since the French and Indian War. Towns formed military units which trained and drilled for battle.

As most people had expected, British officials refused to meet the American demands. The Second Continental Congress was scheduled to meet again in Philadelphia in May 1775 to discuss the next steps. Three weeks before the meeting was to start, war broke out.

THE START OF THE REVOLUTION

The Revolutionary War began in Massachusetts, the scene of so much previous trouble. On the night of April 18, 1775, a large number of British troops headed northwest out of Boston. They had two missions. First, they were to capture the American leaders John Hancock and Sam Adams in the Massachusetts town of Lexington, ten miles northwest of Boston. Second, they were to seize gunpowder in nearby Concord, Massachusetts.

Patriots in Boston discovered the British plans. They sent the Boston silversmith Paul Revere to warn Sam Adams and John Hancock. Thanks to Revere's famous ride, Adams and Hancock escaped from Lexington. Also, about seventy-five men were gathered on Lexington green when the redcoats arrived at dawn on April 19, 1775.

The revolution's first battle was a mass of confusion. The British commander ordered the minutemen, who were really farmers pitted against professional soldiers, to lay down their arms. The outnumbered colonists began running for home. Suddenly someone fired a shot—no one knows from which side—and the British began shooting. Eight minutemen were killed and ten were wounded, while one British soldier was wounded. This first battle of the American Revolution, the Battle of Lexington, was a complete British victory.

Word of the fight at Lexington swept through the Massachusetts countryside. The redcoats who

Currier and Ives engraving of the Minutemen

gathered to destroy the gunpowder at nearby Concord found themselves facing a growing army of enraged Americans. When the British fired on the Americans at Concord's North Bridge, the patriots returned the fire, killing three and wounding eight men. After taking a pounding at the bridge, the British tried to make an orderly retreat to Boston. The Americans kept pace with them, though, and from their hiding places behind trees and farm buildings they picked off the redcoats. By the time the redcoats reached Boston, nearly three hundred of their men had been killed or wounded. The Americans suffered about a hundred men killed or wounded in the running Battle of Concord, which was the first American victory of the war.

On May 10, 1775, just twenty-one days after the Battles of Lexington and Concord, the Second Continental Congress opened in Philadelphia, with Samuel Ward and Stephen Hopkins once again representing Rhode Island. Despite Lexington and Concord, many Congressmen and other Americans still hoped that the problems with Britain could be ironed out. It soon became apparent, however, that a full-scale war was going to be fought.

On June 17, 1775, the Americans and the British clashed in the savage Battle of Bunker Hill near Boston, some five weeks after the Second Continental Congress opened. The British claimed victory in this battle, because they won the hill they sought. However, they lost a thousand men in the process, compared to four hundred for the Americans. Both sides were so bitter about Bunker Hill that few people were in a mood to talk about peace afterwards. The colonists grew even more angry when the king hired thousands of German soldiers, called *Hessians*, to fight them.

Congress knew that America needed good armed services and military leaders to fight

Britain, which was the strongest country in the world at that time. In June 1775 Congress created the Continental Army (now the United States Army) and chose George Washington of Virginia as its Commander in Chief. Thanks in large part to the efforts of Stephen Hopkins of Rhode Island, Congress created the Continental Navy (now the United States Navy) in October 1775. In December of that year, Congress chose the Rhode Islander Esek Hopkins (Stephen's younger brother) as Commander in Chief of the Continental Navy.

Esek Hopkins

While George Washington and Esek Hopkins were building the Army and Navy, Congress was arguing about the independence question. Even as of late 1775, most Americans opposed cutting ties with Britain and forming a new country. Many were scared that America wouldn't be able to stand on its own. Many others felt that, if the colonists declared independence, Britain would punish them all the more after it won the war.

Gradually, however, more and more Americans became convinced that independence was the best course. A book published in January 1776 helped bring about this change in opinion. The book was *Common Sense*, and its author was the English-born Thomas Paine, who had come to live in Philadelphia several years earlier. *Common*

Sense offered reasons why the colonies should free themselves of Britain. Tens of thousands of Americans read *Common Sense* and agreed with Paine's arguments. Americans also realized that, once they declared themselves independent, other countries might help them fight the British.

During the first half of 1776, the governments of the colonies began pushing for independence. In January 1776 New Hampshire became the first of the Thirteen Colonies to form a government completely independent of Britain. On May 4, 1776, by order of its General Assembly, Rhode Island became the first colony to declare itself totally independent of Britain.

On June 7, 1776, the Virginian Richard Henry Lee proposed that the colonies should become "free and independent states" and cut all political ties with Britain. Congress put off a vote on this independence question until July. When Congress voted on the issue after much heated discussion on July 2, 1776, Rhode Island and every other colony but New York chose independence. New York made the vote unanimous by coming out for independence a few days later.

On July 4, 1776, Congress approved a paper explaining why America was cutting its ties with Britain. Fifty-six Congressmen signed this paper,

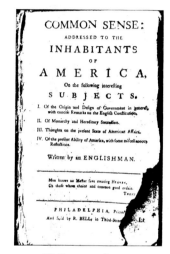

Title page from
Common Sense

Delegates sign the Declaration of Independence

the famous Declaration of Independence,* which had been written by Thomas Jefferson. Stephen Hopkins and William Ellery signed the Declaration for Rhode Island. Ellery had replaced Samuel Ward, who had died in March 1776.

Because the Declaration of Independence was approved on that date, July 4, 1776, has long been considered the birthday of the United States. To make independence a reality would take more than a piece of paper. It would require defeating Britain on the battlefield and on the seas, which for several years seemed very unlikely.

* See Declaration of Independence on page 151

STEPHEN HOPKINS (1707–1785)

Born in Providence, Stephen Hopkins grew up in what is now Scituate, Rhode Island. His mother, who was a Quaker, taught him to read and write. Although he received no formal education, Stephen loved books. When he wasn't working on the family farm, he spent most of his spare hours reading history, law, and poetry. Largely through his own efforts, by the age of 25 he probably was more widely read than most university students of today.

Stephen Hopkins also developed a love for politics. He began what was to be a long political career at age 25 when he was chosen town clerk of Scituate. Hopkins rose higher and higher in Rhode Island politics. First he represented Scituate in the Rhode Island General Assembly and later he represented Providence, where he moved in 1742. He also served many years as governor of Rhode Island and later as the colony's chief justice.

When the *Gaspee* incident took place in 1772, Stephen Hopkins was Rhode Island's chief justice. He opposed the British so strongly that he was not always fair in cases concerning them. As chief justice, he did all he could to make sure that the *Gaspee* raiders were never caught or prosecuted. Other American patriots loved him for this. His enemies said that he had done it because his nephew, John Hopkins (Esek's son), and several other relatives had been among the raiders.

Stephen Hopkins always favored colonial independence, and served as a delegate from Rhode Island to the First and Second Continental Congresses. During the First Continental Congress he gave a thrilling speech about how Americans would have to fight for their rights:

> *Powder and ball will decide this question. The gun and bayonet alone will finish the contest in which we are engaged, and any of you who cannot bring your minds to this mode of adjusting the question had better retire in time.*

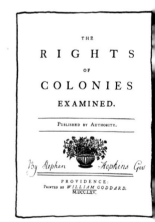

Title page of Hopkins' book

Hopkins made another memorable comment when he signed the Declaration of Independence in 1776. By that time he was nearly 70 years old and suffering from a condition that made his hands shake. He wanted everyone to know that he wasn't trembling out of fear, so as he signed his name he said, "My hand trembles but my heart does not!"

Stephen Hopkins died at the age of 78 in 1785. He had favored a stronger national government. Had he lived just several more years, he might have convinced Rhode Islanders to send delegates to the Constitutional Convention and to approve the Constitution much earlier than they did.

To help the American army, French troops landed in Newport in 1780.

Chapter IX

Winning the Revolution

We fight, get beat, rise, and fight again.

> Nathanael Greene, writing during the
> Revolutionary War

It was often difficult to tell which was more pitiful, the American Army or Navy. George Washington's soldiers lacked guns and bullets. They were not used to following orders, and sometimes said "Do it yourself!" when told to do things by their officers. Congress lacked the money to provide for the soldiers, and as a result there were times when many of them went barefoot and hungry. Seeing that their government could not care for them, soldiers deserted by the hundreds after tough battles or when it was time to harvest the crops. Hundreds grew so disgusted that they switched over to the British side.

To top things off, many Americans, including some members of Congress, questioned why George Washington's army avoided big battles. The reason Washington always seemed to be making small sneak attacks or retreating was that his army might have been slaughtered in a major battle. Some members of Congress who knew little about war thought that George Washington was a poor general and should be replaced. Fortunately, Washington had enough support in government to survive the criticism; and later, when his army was bigger, he went on to lead a decisive victory.

Navy Commander Esek Hopkins was less fortunate. His fleet had only eight vessels that could have fit into a rather small pond. Many of the sailors aboard the fleet were Rhode Islanders, as were many of the officers, including Abraham Whipple. The tiny fleet did very well at first. In early 1776 Esek Hopkins sailed his ships southward to the British-ruled Bahama Islands, where his men captured two forts. Hopkins obtained nearly one hundred cannons and a great deal of ammunition and gunpowder in this victory.

Hopkins and his fleet sailed back toward New London, Connecticut. Just southwest of Rhode Island in Long Island Sound the American fleet captured several British ships. They almost captured an even bigger prize—the British warship *Glasgow*. After a fierce sea battle, the damaged *Glasgow* managed to get away. Nonetheless, the voyage had been very successful, and upon his return Esek Hopkins was hailed as a naval hero—for a while.

Because the pay was higher, most sailors preferred to work as privateers than as Navy sailors. Commander Hopkins tried to get laws passed to curb privateering so that he could recruit more men for the American Navy. This angered some powerful merchants who made a fortune from privateering. In addition, Hopkins was blamed for letting the *Glasgow* escape, and accused of disobeying orders by sailing down to the Bahamas instead of the waters near the Virginia coast as Congress had directed.

Unlike George Washington, Esek Hopkins lost out to his enemies. In early 1778 he was dismissed from the Navy in disgrace, although many people thought that this was completely unfair. During the remainder of the war, privateering vessels were more of a factor in fighting the British than the Continental Navy.

Hundreds of Rhode Island sailors served on privateers that attacked British vessels, and hundreds served in the Continental Navy. Hundreds more fought in the Continental Army. They fought in battles in New York and New Jersey, and in General Nathanael Greene's Southern campaign. No major Revolutionary War

Engraving showing the "Siege of Rhode Island," August 25, 1778

battles were fought in Rhode Island, although the state *almost* hosted a major battle.

In December 1776 a British force of several thousand men under Sir Henry Clinton seized Newport, Rhode Island. Rhode Islanders asked Congress to help them drive the British out of Newport, but Congress had bigger problems to solve at the time. Then in early 1778 France entered the war on the American side. The French saw this as a chance to revenge their loss to Britain during the French and Indian War. As their first joint campaign, the Americans and the French planned to win back Newport from the British.

The plan looked great on paper. A large American force under General John Sullivan of New Hampshire was to attack the British in Newport from the east. A French fleet under Count d'Estaing was to close in on Newport from the west. Together the Americans and the French would drive the British out of Newport.

In summer of 1778 General Sullivan positioned his troops for their assault and Count d'Estaing's fleet approached Newport. Before the Americans and the French could tighten the noose, the British Admiral Richard Howe appeared near Narragansett Bay with a large fleet. The French vessels sailed away from Newport—perhaps to attack the British fleet, perhaps to flee. But a storm came up and smashed both fleets. The British then fled to New York. Instead of helping Sullivan take Newport, Count d'Estaing decided to sail to Boston for ship repairs.

General Sullivan, who was enraged over Count d'Estaing's departure, had his men retreat to the north. During this retreat the Americans met a large body of British troops at Portsmouth, about twelve miles north of Newport on the Island of Rhode Island. At Portsmouth the two sides fought what was called the Battle of Rhode Island on August 29, 1778.

Black troops fought
and died at the Battle
of Rhode Island.

The British reportedly had about three hundred men killed or wounded at this battle, compared to about two hundred losses for the Americans. But despite the fact that it was the state's most important Revolutionary War conflict, the Battle of Rhode Island is considered minor. Sullivan was not able to win back Newport without d'Estaing's help, and his forces had to retreat from Rhode Island once the battle was over. One interesting aspect of the Battle of Rhode Island was that a regiment of black soldiers was in the thick of the fighting against the British.

The British finally left Newport in October 1779 of their own accord. Seeing the tide turning against them, they decided to withdraw their Rhode Island forces to New York. It was said that Newporters flocked to the water's edge and cursed the British as they set sail.

Map of the Battle of Rhode Island

By 1780 the Americans, who had looked like they would lose early in the war, were doing much better. A great Rhode Island general named Nathanael Greene helped bring about the final British downfall. General Greene was placed in charge of the American troops in the South in late 1780. Greene and his troops helped force a huge British army to retreat to Yorktown, Virginia, in summer of 1781, setting the stage for George Washington to make his long-awaited big attack. Washington led his 17,000-man army to Yorktown. While a French fleet closed off escape by sea, Washington's forces cut off escape by land.

Nathanael Greene

For More than a week in October 1781 General Washington's forces pounded their bottled-up enemy with cannons and other heavy guns. British losses mounted, and the ground was so

The British army surrendered at Yorktown, October 19, 1781.

pockmarked from the American shelling that it looked like the craters of the moon in places. After 600 of his men had been killed, the British General Cornwallis surrendered his 8,000 survivors on October 19, 1781.

The great American victory at the Battle of Yorktown, which Nathanael Greene had helped set up, meant that the Americans had won the Revolutionary War. In September 1783 Britain and America signed a peace treaty recognizing that the Thirteen Colonies had become a new country—the United States of America!

ESEK HOPKINS (1718–1802)

Esek Hopkins, Stephen's younger brother, was born at what is now Scituate, Rhode Island. When very young, Esek was given the jobs of gathering firewood and caring for Susanna, the family pig. Esek was taught to read and write a little, but by his teens it was expected that he would become a sailor like several of his older brothers. Shortly after his father's death in 1738, Esek said good-bye to his family and sailed for South America. Within three years he rose from sailor to mate to ship captain and then shipowner.

The Rhode Island Assembly authorized young Esek to send out privateering ships against Spain. One Spanish ship that Esek captured he renamed the *Desire*, after a young lady of Newport named Desire Burroughs. This may have helped him win Desire Burroughs, for she married him in 1741 and later had ten children with him.

During the French and Indian War Esek Hopkins earned a fortune commanding his own privateering fleet. He became famous around Providence, where he and his family had moved into a large house. He even was elected to represent Providence in the Rhode Island Assembly during his land stays.

Because of Esek Hopkins' experience with sea battles, Rhode Island looked to him as a leader once the revolution began. For a few months at the end of 1775 he commanded Rhode Island's land troops but fought in no battles. Partly through the efforts of his brother, Stephen, who was a powerful member of the Continental Congress, late in 1775 Esek was made Commander in Chief of the new Continental Navy.

Shortly after New Year's Day, 1776, Congress ordered Esek Hopkins to sail his eight small ships down to the Virginia coast. He was to learn the strength of the British fleet in the Chesapeake Bay area, and attack it if possible. But his orders also said that in case of problems he was to use his "best judgment" and do what was "most useful to the American cause."

Ice in the Delaware River, where the fleet was anchored, kept Hopkins from departing Philadelphia for weeks. Finally, as crowds along the shore cheered, the little American fleet sailed down the river and entered the open sea on February 17, 1776. Hopkins soon decided to avoid Chesapeake Bay, however. Many of his men were ill from smallpox and two of his ships had been separated from his fleet in a storm. Hopkins thought these problems entitled him to use his "best judgment." Rather than becoming involved in a sea battle with the British fleet, he decided to sail down to the Bahamas and attack the British forts there. This voyage was a great success. Not only did Hopkins and his men obtain valuable war materials in the Bahamas, they captured several British ships on the trip home. However, one powerful ship, the *Glasgow*, blasted its way past the American vessels and escaped. John Hopkins, captain of one of the American ships and Esek's son, was badly wounded in the battle with the *Glasgow*, but recovered.

Esek Hopkins received a hero's welcome upon his return to the colonies in April 1776. Newspaper articles and poems were written about him, and John Hancock, the president of the Continental Congress, wrote him a letter of congratulations. However, some powerful people turned against Esek Hopkins because of his campaign against privateering. Soon he found himself blamed for going down to the Bahamas instead of the Virginia coast and for letting the *Glasgow* escape. Hopkins had some powerful friends in Congress, including future United States President John Adams, who thought he had done "great service." However, in January 1778 Congress dismissed Hopkins from the Navy.

Esek Hopkins was bitter about the injustice done him but continued to serve his country as best he could. Still quite popular in Rhode Island, he was elected to the state's General Assembly in 1777 and served there for about ten years. Esek Hopkins, who might have led the American Navy to great victories had he been given the chance, died at the age of 83 in North Providence, Rhode Island.

ABRAHAM WHIPPLE (1733-1819)

Born at Providence, Abraham Whipple was a descendant of one of the first settlers of the town. Abraham went off to sea as a boy, and soon became an expert sailor. During the French and Indian War he commanded a privateer that captured twenty-three French ships on a six-month voyage in 1759-1760.

Long before the revolution actually began, Whipple wholeheartedly took the patriots' side. In 1772 he led the attack on the *Gaspee* and Lieutenant Dudingston. Whipple and the other raiders escaped punishment because Rhode Islanders refused to speak out against them.

After the Lexington and Concord battles in spring of 1775, Rhode Island sent out two ships under Abraham Whipple to protect Rhode Island shipping. In a skirmish that is sometimes called the first sea battle ot the revolution, Whipple captured a small boat belonging to the British ship *Rose* near Newport. The *Rose*'s captain wrote Whipple a note saying that he knew he had been involved in the *Gaspee* burning and that he would hang him. Abraham Whipple wrote back a short, sarcastic response:

> *Sir James Wallace, always catch a man before you hang him.*
> ABRAHAM WHIPPLE

Abraham Whipple was captain of one of the ships in Esek Hopkins' small fleet and helped capture the two forts in the Bahamas and the British ships near Long Island. Like Esek Hopkins, Whipple was criticized for allowing the *Glasgow* to escape. But Congress found him not guilty of any wrongdoing, except for acting "rough" with his officers.

Congress sent Captain Whipple out with other ships during the remainder of the war. He was captain of the *Providence*, which reportedly captured more British vessels during the war than had any other American ship. After the *Providence* was captured by the enemy, Whipple was given command of a new ship, also named the *Providence*. At one point when the British had the new *Providence* and other American ships bottled up in Narragansett Bay, Whipple blasted his way out. He then carried important messages from the American government to France, where he met the king.

In 1779, while commanding the new *Providence*, Whipple proved that he was smart as well as tough. That July he encountered a fleet of nearly 150 British merchant ships on their way from Jamaica to Britain. This huge fleet was escorted by gunships, so Whipple could not fire on it. Instead he hid his ship's guns, raised the British flag, and joined the British fleet as though his ship were part of it.

During the next several nights Whipple sent armed men out to board and capture nearby ships of this fleet. Whipple's crew seized eleven ships this way. Then, breaking away from the British fleet, the *Providence* headed home with its captured ships. The goods on the eight enemy vessels that reached the American shore were reportedly worth a million dollars, making this one of the richest sea captures of the revolution.

Whipple soon sailed to defend Charleston, South Carolina. When the British captured Charleston in 1780, the *Providence* was also captured and Whipple was imprisoned. The war was almost over, though, and Whipple was soon freed. After the war, he lived for several years on his farm near Cranston, Rhode Island. In 1788 the great sea captain and adventurer moved to a farm in Ohio, where he lived to the age of 85.

NATHANAEL GREENE (1742–1786)

Nathanael Greene was born in Potowomut (part of Warwick), Rhode Island, into a Quaker family. No schools existed as yet in Nathanael's town, so his father hired a traveling tutor to teach Nathanael and his brothers a little reading, writing, and math. Although Nathanael yearned for more schooling, his father told him to forget the idea and concentrate on his work at the family farm and ironworks.

Nathanael found ways to learn on his own. He borrowed books from his uncle, a Warwick judge, and read them when he wasn't busy making iron or farming. He also made little anchors and other iron and wooden toys which he sold in Newport. He used the money to buy books at a Newport bookstore.

Nathanael wasn't only a bookworm. Although his parents frowned on such activities, Nathanael loved dances and parties. He found a way to get around his parents' rules. He would go up into his room, supposedly to read or sleep. Minutes later he would climb out his bedroom window down to the ground, and then head to the party or dance.

In 1770 Nathanael moved to Coventry, Rhode Island, to run the family's ironworks there. That same year he was elected to the Rhode Island General Assembly. One of his first acts as a Rhode Island lawmaker was to found a school for the town's children.

Nathanael Greene wanted to be prepared in case the turmoil with Britain turned to war. In spring of 1773 he attended a military meeting in Connecticut. However, the Quakers disapproved of war and expelled him from the Society of Friends for going to the meeting. In 1774, the year he got married, Nathanael Greene helped form a volunteer military group called the Kentish Guards. Because he had a limp, the other Guards allowed Nathanael only the rank of private. Nathanael Greene thought this was unfair, but he did all he could to help the Guards anyway. He read every book he could find on warfare to increase his knowledge of the subject. He also went to Boston where he hired a British army deserter to train the Kentish Guards.

A few days after the Battles of Lexington and Concord, many people were shocked to learn that the Rhode Island General Assembly had chosen Nathanael Greene to lead the 1,500-man army it was raising. Thanks to the ability he had displayed and his willingness to do anything to help, Nathanael had instantly risen from a low-ranking Kentish Guardsman to general of Rhode Island's main army!

In late spring of 1775 Greene and his troops joined a large American army that was penning up the redcoats at Boston. George Washington, who arrived in the Boston area in early July 1775 to take command of the entire American army, liked Greene from the start. Soon Greene was promoted to general in the Continental Army and was commanding men from other colonies besides Rhode Island.

General Nathanael Greene served in many key Revolutionary War battles and operations. He helped Washington drive the British from Boston in March 1776, then commanded the American soldiers who occupied the city. During the first bleak years of the war, he led troops in battles in New York, New Jersey, and Pennsylvania. Washington was impressed by Greene's ability to plan out battles, make good decisions under fire, and motivate his men. In fact, it was widely known that George Washington wanted Greene to take his place as Commander in Chief of the Continental Army in case he was killed.

Nathanael Greene enjoyed his finest hours after George Washington named him to command the Southern Army in October 1780. Leading his men in heroic battles in North and South Carolina, Greene helped drive British General Cornwallis's army to Yorktown, Virginia, where it was beaten by Washington's forces. For doing so much to free the Southern states from British control, Greene was called the "Savior of the South."

The great Rhode Island general had financial problems during his last years, partly because he had spent his own money on his troops. Often called the greatest American general of the revolution besides George Washington, Nathanael Greene died at the age of 43 only three years after the war ended.

State House, Newport, Rhode Island

Chapter X

The Thirteenth State!

[Rhode Island] was the first colony to instruct her delegates against the stamp act . . . the first colony to call for a Continental Congress in 1774, and the earliest to elect her delegates to this first Continental Congress; [it was also] the colony in which the first overt act of resistance to Great Britain had occurred. . . . This state, with so preeminently distinguished a record, would not have been the last to [approve] the constitution of the United States, had Stephen Hopkins lived. . . .

From Stephen Hopkins, a Rhode Island Statesman, *by William E. Foster*

Coat of Arms of Rhode Island

Seal of the State

In its first years, the United States was governed by the Articles of Confederation, which went into effect in spring of 1781 and remained the law of the land until the United States Constitution went into effect seven years later. The Articles created a weak central government for the United States, while allowing each state to be very strong. That was the way most Americans wanted things. The states had banded together to win the revolution, but afterward most people went back to thinking of their state as more important than the country as a whole. In addition, most people were afraid that a strong central government would tax them highly and have too much control over their lives.

The result was that the United States was very weak in its early years. The country had no president to lead it and no federal courts. Because the federal government was not allowed to levy taxes, it had to beg the states for money. Since the states gave the federal government only a fraction of the money it needed, the country could not pay its debts.

Congress could not even pay the soldiers who had helped win the revolution. As time passed and the government did not pay its IOU's, many of the soldiers grew angry. In summer of 1783, a group of army veterans seeking their back pay marched on the building where the national lawmakers were meeting in Philadelphia. To avoid trouble, the Congressmen ran off to Princeton, New Jersey, which then replaced Philadelphia as the nation's capital.

The lack of a permanent capital during the country's first twenty-five years caused many problems. People who wanted to write to their national lawmakers often did not know where to find them. Lawmakers would head to a city they thought was the capital, only to learn that the government had moved. Between 1776 and the year 1800, when Washington, D.C., became the permanent site, eight different cities served as the nation's capital.

The quality of the men in the national government was an even greater problem than the lack of a permanent meeting place. Most good lawmakers preferred to serve in the state rather than in the national government in the country's early years. There was a big attendance problem in Congress. On some days so few Congressmen showed up that all they could do was chat and drink tea instead of making badly needed laws.

There were still other problems at the state level. In many cases the states did not get along with each other. New Jersey and Connecticut argued with New York over financial matters. Maryland and Virginia argued over the use of the Potomac River. The U.S. government could not settle these disputes because in many ways each state alone was more powerful than the entire national government! To make matters worse, the 1780s were rough financially for many people. The decade was marked by economic depressions —times when people have less money than usual.

Despite this long list of problems, until 1786 most Americans continued to believe that a strong federal government was a greater evil than a weak, disorganized one. Several events in 1786 changed public opinion. One was Shays' Rebellion, a revolt by farmers in western Massachusetts that took place from fall of 1786 to early 1787. Daniel Shays and his followers were fighting for lower taxes in Massachusetts and an end to the jailing of people who owed large sums of money. The federal government, which had just a 700-man army, was too weak to put down this revolt, so the Massachusetts militia had to do it. People began to wonder: Would the country be ripped apart by a series of rebellions?

Thus, by early 1787 most Americans favored a stronger central government, although quite a few people still opposed the idea. Rhode Island as a whole argued against it for several reasons. Rhode Islanders feared that the large states would control the central government, leaving the small ones powerless. They also were afraid that a strong central government would interfere with their state's shipping and trading businesses. In addition, Rhode Islanders had controlled most of their own affairs even in colonial times, and they were not ready to be told what to do by outsiders.

To create a stronger federal government, a national convention was held in Philadelphia, Pennsylvania, from May to September 1787. Twelve states sent delegates to this Constitutional Convention. Only Rhode Island refused to send delegates.

George Washington presided over the meetings of the Constitutional Convention.

Handwritten notes recorded the issues and the number of votes each one received.

The convention created a new set of national laws for the country—The United States Constitution. Each of the ex-colonies was already a state, but a state under the Articles of Confederation. Each would become a state under the Constitution when it approved the new document. The Constitution itself would become the law of the country once nine states had approved it.

Delaware became the first state when it approved the Constitution on December 7, 1787. The Constitution went into effect when New Hampshire, the ninth state, approved it on June 21, 1788. The remaining four states—Virginia, New York, North Carolina, and Rhode Island—

were actually foreign states outside the United States at that point. Virginia and New York joined the country by approving the Constitution within several days of New Hampshire. When North Carolina approved the Constitution in late 1789, that left only the smallest state, Rhode Island, outside the country.

The federal government threatened to take actions against Rhode Island that would cost the state money, but still Rhode Island would not join the other twelve states. One thing Rhode Islanders wanted added to the Constitution was a Bill of Rights guaranteeing certain basic rights to individuals. By 1790 Congress had created a Bill of Rights. Over time more and more Rhode Islanders favored the Constitution. At one point, Providence even threatened to leave Rhode Island and join the country by itself. In March 1790 a

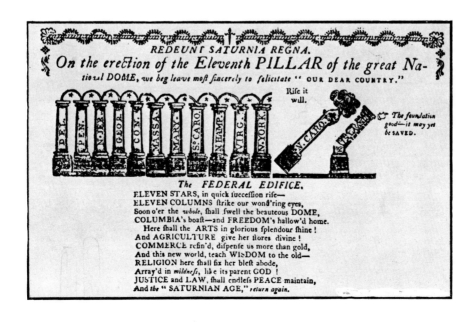

REDEUNT SATURNIA REGNA.
On the erection of the Eleventh PILLAR of the great National DOME, we beg leave most sincerely to felicitate "OUR DEAR COUNTRY."

Rise it will.

The foundation good—it may yet be SAVED.

The FEDERAL EDIFICE.
ELEVEN STARS, in quick succession rise—
ELEVEN COLUMNS strike our wond'ring eyes,
Soon o'er the whole, shall swell the beauteous DOME,
COLUMBIA's boast—and FREEDOM's hallow'd home.
Here shall the ARTS in glorious splendour shine!
And AGRICULTURE give her stores divine!
COMMERCE refin'd, dispense us more than gold,
And this new world, teach WISDOM to the old—
RELIGION here shall fix her blest abode,
Array'd in mildness, like its parent GOD!
JUSTICE and LAW, shall endless PEACE maintain,
And the "SATURNIAN AGE," return again.

The BILL of RIGHTS, and AMENDMENTS to the CONSTITUTION OF THE UNITED STATES, as agreed to by the CONVENTION of the State of *Rhode-Island and Providence-Plantations*, at *South-Kingstown*, in the County of *Washington*, on the First *Monday* of *March*, A. D. 1790.

DECLARATION of RIGHTS.

1. THAT there are certain natural rights, of which men, when they form a social compact, cannot deprive or divest their posterity—among which are the enjoyment of life and liberty, with the means of acquiring, possessing and protecting property, and pursuing and obtaining happiness and safety.

2. That all power is naturally vested in and consequently derived from the people: That magistrates, therefore, are their trustees and agents, and at all times amenable to them.

3. That the powers of government may be reassumed by the people, whensoever it shall become necessary to their happiness:—That the rights of the States respectively to nominate and appoint all State officers, and every other power, jurisdiction and right, which is not by the said Constitution clearly delegated to the Congress of the United States, or to the departments of government thereof, remain to the people of the several States, or their respective State governments, to whom they may have granted the same;—and that those clauses in the said Constitution, which declare that Congress shall not have or exercise certain powers, do not imply, that Congress is entitled to any powers not given by the said Constitution;—but such clauses are to be construed, either as exceptions to certain specified powers, or as inserted merely for greater caution.

4. That religion, or the duty which we owe to our Creator, and the manner of discharging it, can be directed only by reason and conviction, not by force or violence—and therefore all men have an equal, natural and unalienable right to the free exercise of religion, according to the dictates of conscience—and that no particular religious sect, or society, ought to be favoured or established by law, in preference to others.

5. That the legislative, executive and judiciary powers of government, should be separate and distinct;—and that the members of the two first may be restrained from oppression, by feeling and participating the public burthens, they should at fixed periods be reduced to a private station, return into the mass of the people, and the vacancies be supplied by certain and regular elections—in which all or any part of the former members to be eligible or ineligible, as the rules of the Constitution of government and the laws shall direct.

6. That elections of Representatives in the Legislature ought to be free and frequent—and all men, having sufficient evidence of permanent common interest with and attachment to the community, ought to have the right of suffrage: And no aid, charge, tax or fee, can be set, rated or levied upon the people, without their own consent, or that of their Representatives, so elected;—nor can they be bound by any law, to which they have not, in like manner, assented for the public good.

7. That all power of suspending laws, or the execution of laws, by any authority, without the consent of the Representatives of the people in the Legislature, is injurious to their rights, and ought not to be exercised.

8. That in all capital and criminal prosecutions, a man hath a right to demand the cause and nature of his accusation—to be confronted with the accusers and witnesses—to call for evidence, and be allowed counsel in his favour—and to a fair and speedy trial by an impartial jury of his vicinage, without whose unanimous consent he cannot be found guilty (except in the government of the land and naval forces) nor can he be compelled to give evidence against himself.

9. That no freeman ought to be taken, imprisoned, or disseized of his freehold, liberties, privileges or franchises, or outlawed, or exiled, or in any manner destroyed, or deprived of his life, liberty or property, but by the trial by jury, or by the law of the land.

10. That every freeman restrained of his liberty is entitled to a remedy, to enquire into the lawfulness thereof, and to remove the same, if unlawful;—and that such remedy ought not to be denied or delayed.

11. That in controversies respecting property, and in suits between man and man, the ancient trial by jury, as hath been exercised by us and our ancestors, from the time whereof the memory of man is not to the contrary, is one of the greatest securities to the rights of the people, and ought to remain sacred and inviolate.

12. That every freeman ought to obtain right and justice freely, and without sale—completely, and without denial—promptly, and without delay—and that all establishments or regulations, contravening these rights, are oppressive and unjust.

13. That excessive bail ought not to be required, nor excessive fines imposed; nor cruel or unusual punishments inflicted.

14. That every person has a right to be secure from all unreasonable searches and seizures of his person, his papers, or his property; and therefore that all warrants to search suspected places, or seize any person, his papers, or his property, without information upon oath, or affirmation of sufficient cause, are grievous and oppressive;—and that all general warrants (or such in which the place or person suspected are not particularly designated) are dangerous, and ought not to be granted.

15. That the people have a right peaceably to assemble together, to consult for their common good, or to instruct their Representatives; and that every person has a right to petition, or apply to the Legislature, for redress of grievances.

16. That the people have a right to freedom of speech, and of writing and publishing their sentiments:—That freedom of the press is one of the greatest bulwarks of liberty, and ought not to be violated.

17. That the people have a right to keep and bear arms:—That a well regulated militia, including the body of the people capable of bearing arms, is the proper, natural and safe defence of a free State:—That the militia shall not be subject to martial law, except in time of war, rebellion or insurrection. That standing armies in time of peace are dangerous to liberty, and ought not to be kept up, except in cases of necessity; and that at all times the military should be under strict subordination to the civil power:—That in time of peace no soldier ought to be quartered in any house without the consent of the owner—and in time of war, only by the civil magistrate, in such manner as the law directs.

18. That any person religiously scrupulous of bearing arms, ought to be exempted, upon payment of an equivalent to employ another to bear arms in his stead.

AMENDMENTS to the CONSTITUTION of the UNITED STATES.

1. THE United States shall guarantee to each State its sovereignty, freedom and independence, and every power, jurisdiction and right, which is not by this Constitution expressly delegated to the United States.

2. That Congress shall not alter, modify or interfere, in the times, places and manner, of holding elections for Senators and Representatives, or either of them, except when the Legislature of any State shall neglect, refuse, or be disabled, by invasion or rebellion, to prescribe the same;—or in case when the provision made by the States is so imperfect, as that no consequent election is had;—and then only, until the Legislature of such State shall make provision in the premises.

3. It is declared by the Convention, that the judicial power of the United States, in cases in which a State may be a party, does not extend to criminal prosecutions, or to authorize any suit by any person against a State—but, to remove all doubts or controversies respecting the same, that it be especially expressed as a part of the Constitution of the United States, that Congress shall not, directly or indirectly, either by themselves or through the judiciary, interfere with any one of the States in the redemption of paper money already emitted, and now in circulation, or in liquidating and discharging the public securities of any one State:—That each and every State shall have the exclusive right of making such laws and regulations for the before mentioned purposes, as they shall think proper.

4. That no amendments to the Constitution of the United States hereafter to be made, pursuant to the fifth article, shall take effect, or become a part of the Constitution of the United States, after the year 1793, without the consent of eleven of the States heretofore united under one Confederation.

5. That the judicial powers of the United States shall extend to no possible case, where the cause or action shall have originated before the ratification of this Constitution, except in disputes between States about their territory—disputes between persons claiming lands under grants of different States—and debts due to the United States.

6. That no person shall be compelled to do military duty, otherwise than by voluntary enlistment, except in cases of general invasion; any thing in the second paragraph of the sixth article of the Constitution, or any law made under the Constitution, to the contrary notwithstanding.

7. That no capitation or poll-tax shall ever be laid by Congress.

8. In cases of direct taxes, Congress shall first make requisitions on the several States, to assess, levy and pay, their respective proportions of such requisitions, in such way and manner as the Legislatures of the several States shall judge best. And in case any State shall neglect or refuse to pay its proportion, pursuant to such requisition, then Congress may assess and levy such State's proportion, together with interest at the rate of six per cent. per annum, from the time prescribed in such requisition.

9. That Congress shall lay no direct taxes, without the consent of the Legislatures of three-fourths of the States in the Union.

10. That the journals of the proceedings of the Senate and House of Representatives shall be published, as soon as conveniently may be, at least once in every year, except such parts thereof, relating to treaties, alliances, or military operations, as in their judgment require secrecy.

11. That the regular statement and account of the receipts and expenditures of all public money shall be published at least once in every year.

12. As standing armies in time of peace are dangerous to liberty, and ought not to be kept up, except in cases of necessity; and as at all times the military should be under strict subordination to the civil power——that therefore no standing army or regular troops, shall be raised or kept up in time of peace.

13. That no monies be borrowed on the credit of the United States, without the assent of two-thirds of the Senators and Representatives present in each House.

14. That the Congress shall not declare war, without the concurrence of two-thirds of the Senators and Representatives present in each House.

15. That the words " without the consent of Congress," in the seventh clause, in the ninth section of the first article of the Constitution, be expunged.

16. That no Judge of the Supreme Court of the United States shall hold any other office under the United States, or any of them; nor shall any officer appointed by Congress be permitted to hold any office under the appointment of any of the States.

17. As a traffic tending to establish or continue the slavery of any part of the human species, is disgraceful to the cause of liberty and humanity—that Congress shall, as soon as may be, promote and establish such laws and regulations as may effectually prevent the importation of slaves of every description into the United States.

18. And that the amendments proposed by Congress, in March, A. D. 1789, be adopted by this Convention, except the second article therein contained.

In CONVENTION, *March* 6, 1790.
VOTED, That the Bill of Rights and Amendments, proposed to the Federal Constitution, be referred to the Freemen of the several towns, at their meetings on the Third Wednesday of April next, for their consideration: That one copy thereof be sent to each Town-Clerk in this State, one to each Member of the Convention, and one to each Member of the Upper and Lower Houses of Assembly; and that they be sent to the Sheriffs of the several Counties, to be distributed.

The foregoing is a true Copy.

By Order of the Convention,

DANIEL UPDIKE, *Secretary.*

A 1790 newspaper printed the Bill of Rights.

Rhode Island convention met in South Kingston to decide whether to approve the Constitution. There was so much bickering at this meeting that it ended without reaching a decision.

A second convention met at Newport in May 1790. Finally, by the slimmest of margins—34 to 32—this convention voted to approve the Constitution on May 29, 1790! On that day little Rhode Island became the last of the thirteen original states to join the country under its new Constitution.

George Washington, who had been elected first President of the United States in 1789, decided to visit Rhode Island to welcome the little state into the Union. President Washington made the

George and Martha Washington visit Rhode Island.

This 1790 broadside announced Washington's arrival.

journey with several other well-known statesmen, including Thomas Jefferson. When he arrived in Providence in August 1790, Washington was greeted by huge crowds, ringing church bells, and cannon salutes. Washington's visit to the smallest state proved to be a wise move. It helped cement relations between the country as a whole and the stubborn little state that had been the first to declare itself independent from Britain but the last to approve the Constitution.

The village of Providence, Rhode Island looking southwest from Benefit
Street near the head of Goal Lane.

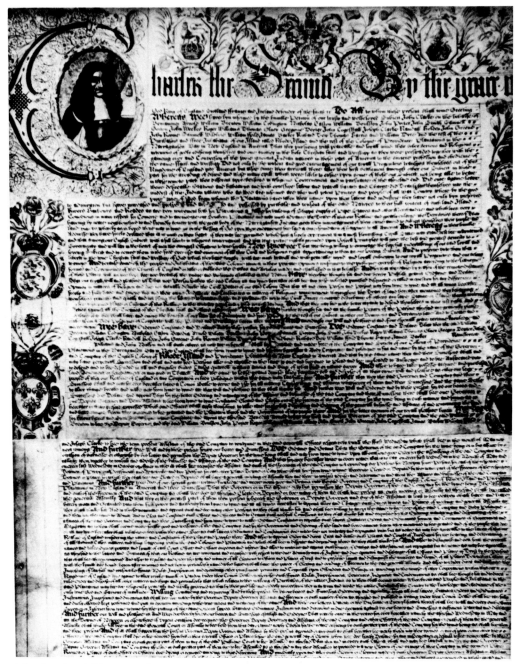

Rhode Island Charter of 1663

A
PROCLAMATION

Bʸ The *PRESIDENT* and *COUNCIL* of His Majeſtiy's Territory & Dominion of *NEW-ENGLAND* in AMERICA.

WHEREAS His Moſt Excellent Majeſty our Soveraign LORD *JAMES* the Second, King of *England, Scotland, France* and *Ireland,* Defender of the Faith &c. by COMMISSION or *Letters Patents* under His Great Seal of *England,* bearing Date the Eight day of *October in* the firſt , ~ of His Reign hath been gracioully pleaſed to erect and conſtitute a PRESIDENT and COUNCIL to take Care of all *that* His Territory and Dominion of *New-England* called the *Maſſachuſets Bay,* the Provinces of *New-Hampſhire* & *Main,* and the *Narraganſet Countrey,* otherwiſe called the *Kings-Province,* with all the Iſlands, Rights and Members thereunto appertaining; and to Order Rule and GOVERN the ſame according to the Rules, Methods and Regulations ſpecified in the ſaid *Commiſſion:* Together with His Majeſties Gracious *Indulgence* in matters of *Religion.*

And for the Execution of His Royal pleaſure in that behalf, His Majeſty hath been pleaſed to appoint *Joſeph Dudley* Eſq to be the firſt *PRESIDENT* of His Majeſties ſaid *Council,* & *VICE-ADMIRAL* of theſe Seas. And to Continue in the ſaid Offices until his Majeſty ſhall otherwiſe direct, & alſo to nominate & appoint *William Stoughton,* Eſq: now *Deputy-Preſident, Simon Bradſtreet, Robert Maſon, John Fitz-Winthrope, John Pynchon, Peter Bulkley, Edward Randolph, Wait Winthrope, Richard Wharton, John Uſher, Nathaniel Saltonſtal, Bartholomew Gidney, Jonathan Tyng, Dudley Bradſtreet, John Hinks,* and *Edward Tyng,* Eſq's: &c, be His Majeſties *Council* in the ſaid *Colony* and Territories.

The *Preſident* & *Council* therefore being convened and having according to the Direction & Form of the ſaid Commiſſion, taken their Oathes and Entered the GOVERNMENT aforeſaid ; and finding it needful, that ſpeedy & effectual Care be taken for the Obſervation of His Majeſties Commands, and particularly for the Regulation and good Government of the *Narraganſet* Countrey or *Kings-Province,* which hath hitherto been *unſetled.* They the ſaid *Preſident* & *Council* have reſolved ſpeedily to *erect* and *ſetle* a conſtant *Court* of *Record* upon the place ; and that the *Preſident, Deputy-Preſident,* or ſome others of the Members of His Majeſties *Council* ſhall be preſent to give all neceſſary Power and Directions for *Eſtabliſhing* His Majeſties. *Government* there, and Adminiſtration of Juſtice to *All* His Majeſties Subjects within the ſaid *Narraganſet Countrey* or *Kings-Province,* and all the *Iſlands, Rights,* and *Members* thereof. And the ſaid *Preſident* & *Council* have in the interim aſſigned *Richard Smith* Eſq : *James Pendleton,* and *John Fones* Gentlemen, *Juſtices* to keep the *Peace* of our Soveraign Lord the KING and all His Subjects : And alſo given Commiſſion to the ſaid *Richard Smith* to be *Sergeant Major,* and Chief Commander of His Majeſties *Militia,* both of *Horſe* & *Foot* within the *Narraganſet Countrey* or *Province,* and all the Iſlands Rights and Members thereof. THEREFORE the ſaid *Preſident* & *Council* doe hereby in His Majeſties Name and by virtue of His ſaid Commiſſion ſtrictly Require & Command all other perſons *being or coming* upon the place, to forbear the Exerciſe of all manner of Juriſdiction, Authority, and Power, and to ceaſe all further Proceedings for the Allotments or Diviſions of Land, or making any *Strip* or *Waſte* upon any part of the ſaid Province, ſave only on each man's *ſtated* Propriety, except by Licence obtained from the ſaid Court, or the *Preſident* & *Council,* until there ſhall be ſuch effectual Regulation and Government eſtabliſhed as is directed by His Majeſty. And the ſaid *Preſident* & *Council* doe hereby henceforth *diſcharge* all His Majeſties Subjects within the ſaid *Narraganſet Countrey* or *Kings Province* and all the Iſlands, Rights & Members thereof *from* the Government of the *Governour* & *Company* of *Connecticut* & *Rhode-Iſland* and *Providence* Plantation, & all others pretending any Power or Juriſdiction. Hereby Charging & Commanding all His Majeſties Subjects to yeild ready & due *Obedience* to the ſaid *Juſtices* of the Peace, the *Sergeant Major* or Cheif Commander of His Majeſties *Militia.* And *George Weightman, Thomas Eldridge, Thomas Monford* and *William Chaplin* are hereby appointed & authorized preſent Conſtables: and Liberty given to the aforeſaid Juſtices to appoint ſo many more as they ſhall ſee needful to them, and to adminiſter Oathes unto the aforeſaid Conſtables & ſuch as are to be Ordeined. And all other perſons are to be *aiding* & *aſſiſting* unto them the ſaid Juſtices and Conſtables in the Execution and Diſcharge of their reſpective Offices, Charges and Truſts, as they will anſwer the contrary at their utmoſt Peril. *Given from the* Council-houſe *in* Boſton *this 28th Day of May Anno Domini 1686. Annoq: Regni Regis* Jacobi Secundi *ſecundo.*

By the Preſident and Council,   *Edward Randolph* Secc't

GOD SAVE THE KING

BOSTON, in N. E. *Printed by* Richard Pierce, *Printer to the Honourable His Majeſties Preſident and Council of this Government.*

Proclamation by the President and Council of New England, May 28, 1686

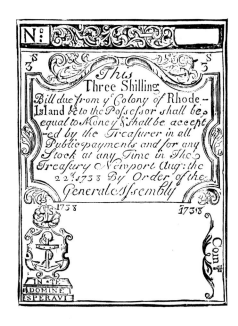

Currency issued by Rhode Island

This Indenture, WITNESSETH,

That John Andrew Esqr and mess.rs Jonathan Olney Barzillai Richmond Isaiah Hawkins William Pearce and Samuel Currie who constitute and make the Town Council of the Town of Providence in the County of Provid: in the Colony of Rhodesland, in their said capacity ——————

hath put ——— and by these Presents, doth voluntarily, ~~and of~~ ~~and freely, and with the Consent of~~ ~~cause free Will~~ put and bind ~~putter~~ Phebe Smith an Infant und the age of Twenty one years, who is a poor Child of said Town ~~put an Infant~~ An ——— Apprentice to Eleazer Green of said Providence and to h. Heirs Executors and Administrators

to learn the Art, Trade, or Mystery of HouseWife, and with him or them ~~after~~ after the Manner of an Apprentice, to serve from the Day of the Date hereof ——— ——— next ensuing, to be compleat and ended. During all which said Term, the said Apprentice her said master ——— ——— faithfully shall serve, his Secrets keep, his lawful Commands gladly obey: Shee shall do no Damage to her said Master ——— nor see it done by others, without letting or giving Notice thereof to her said Master ——— Shee shall not waste her said Masters ——— Goods, nor lend them unlawfully to any. Shee shall not commit Fornication, nor contract Matrimony within the said Term. At Cards, Dice, or any other unlawful Game, She shall not play, whereby her said Master ——— ——— may have Damage, with his own Goods, or the Goods of others: She shall not absent her self ——— by Day or by Night, from her said Masters ——— Service, without his ——— Leave; or haunt Ale-houses, Taverns, or Play-houses; but in all Things behave her self ——— as a good and faithful Apprentice ought to do, towards her said master ——— and all his ——— during the said Term. And the said Master for him Selfhis heirs Executors &c doth hereby promise to teach and instruct, or cause the said Apprentice to be taught and instructed in the Art, Trade, or Calling of a Housewife by the best Ways and Means doe ——— can. and also find and provide for said apprentice Good and Sufficient meat Drink apparrel washing and Lodging with all other necessaries both in Sickness and in helth, fitting for Such an apprentice during said Term and a To Teach her to Read and Write English within said Term if Capable and at the Expire thereof to Give unto said apprentice one Good new Suite of Apparrel for all parts of body fitting for Such an apprentice, besides her Common Wearing Clothes and to formally Dismiss her from this Indenture, In further Consideration of which the said master acknowledges himself to have Received of the overseers of the poor for said Town of Providence the sum of Two hundred and fifty pounds olde Tenor as a ~~prem~~ premium for Takeing said apprentice

IN TESTIMONY whereof, the Parties to these Presents, have hereunto inter-changeably set their Hands and Seals, the ——— Day of July in the 34th ——— Year of the Reign of Our Sovereign Lord George The Second ——— King of Great-Britain, &c. Annoq; Dom. 1760 ———

Signed, Sealed, and Delivered, in the Presence of

Danll Marsh

William Barker

Eleazer Green

Legal document of indentured servants dated July 1760

L. S.

GEORGE R.

By the KING.

A PROCLAMATION:

FOR the difcovering and apprehending the Perfons who plundered and burnt the *Gafpee* Schooner ; and barbaroufly wounded and ill treated Lieutenant *William Dudingfton*, Commander of the faid Schooner.

WHEREAS We have received Information, that upon the 10th Day of June laft, between the Hours of Twelve and One in the Morning, in the Providence or Natrowganfet River, in Our Colony of Rhode-Ifland and Providence Plantations, a great Number of Perfons, armed with Guns and other offenfive Weapons, and led by Two Perfons, who were called the Captain and Head-Sheriff, in feveral armed Boats, attacked and Boarded Our Veffel called the Gafpee Schooner, then lying at fingle Anchor in the faid River, commanded by Our Lieutenant William Dudington, under the Orders of Our Rear-Admiral John Montagu, and having dangeroufly wounded and barbaroufly treated the faid William Dudingfton, took, plundered and burnt the faid Schooner :

WE, to the Intent that fuch outrageous and heinous Offenders may be difcovered, and brought to condign Punifhment have thought fit, with the Advice of Our Privy Council, to iffue this Our Royal PROCLAMATION : And We are hereby gracioufly pleafed to promife, that if any Perfon or Perfons fhall difcover any other Perfor or Perfons concerned in the faid daring and heinous Offences, above mentioned, fo that he or they may be apprehended and brought to Juftice, fuch Difcoverer fhall have and receive, as a Reward for fuch Difcovery, upon Conviction of each of the faid Offenders, the Sum of *Five Hundred Pounds*. And if any Perfon or Perfons fhall difcover either of the faid Perfons who acted as, or called themfelves, or were called by their faid Accomplices, the Head-Sheriff or the Captain, fo that they, or either of them, may be apprehended and brought to Punifhment, fuch Difcoverer fhall have and receive, as a Reward for fuch Difcovery, upon Conviction of either of the faid Perfons, the further Sum of *Five Hundred Pounds*, over and above the Sum of *Five Hundred Pounds* herein before promifed, for the difcovery & apprehending any of the other common Offenders, abovementioned ; and if any Perfon or Perfons concerned therein, except the Two Perfons who were called the Head-Sheriff, and Captain, and the Perfon or Perfons who wounded Our faid Lieutenant *William Dudingfton*, fhall difcover any one or more of the faid Accomplices, fo that he or they may be apprehended and brought to Punifhment, fuch Difcoverer fhall have and receive the faid Reward or Rewards of *Five Hundred Pounds*, or *One Thoufand Pounds*, as the Cafe may be ; and alfo Our gracious Pardon for his faid Offence. And the Commiffioners for executing the Office of Treafurer of Our Exchequer, are hereby required to make Payment accordingly of the faid Rewards. And We do hereby ftrictly charge and command all Our Governors, Deputy-Governors, Magiftrates, Officers, and all other Our Loving Subjects, that they do ufe their utmoft Diligence in their feveral Places and Capacities, to find out, difcover and apprehend the faid Offenders, in Order to their being brought to Juftice. And We do hereby command that this Our Proclamation be printed and publifhed, in the ufual Form, and affixed in the principal Places of Our Town of Newport, and other Towns in Our faid Colony, that none may pretend Ignorance.

GIVEN at Our Court at St. James's, the Twenty-Sixth Day of Auguft, 1772, in the Twelfth Year of Our Reign.

G O D fave the K I N G.

Printed by SOLOMON SOUTHWICK, Printer to the Honorable the Governor and Company of the Colony of Rhode-Ifland and Providence Plantations, in New-England.

Proclamation of George III offering a reward for the capture of those colonists who took part in the burning of the *Gaspee*.

In CONGRESS, July 4, 1776

The unanimous Declaration of the thirteen united States of America.

The Declaration of Independence

Colonial America Time Line

Before the arrival of Europeans, many millions of Indians belonging to dozens of tribes lived in North America (and also in Central and South America)

About A.D. 982—Eric the Red, born in Norway, reaches Greenland during one of the first European voyages to North America

About 985—Eric the Red brings settlers from Iceland to Greenland

About 1000—Leif Eriksson (Eric the Red's son) leads what is thought to be the first European expedition to mainland North America; Leif probably lands in Canada

1492—Christopher Columbus, sailing for Spain, reaches America

1497—John Cabot reaches Canada in the first English voyage to North America

1513—Ponce de León of Spain explores Florida

1519-1521—Hernando Cortés of Spain conquers Mexico

1565—St. Augustine, Florida, the first permanent European town in what is now the United States, is founded by the Spanish

1607—Jamestown, Virginia is founded, the first permanent English town in the present-day U.S.

1608—Frenchman Samuel de Champlain founds the village of Quebec, Canada

1609—Henry Hudson explores the eastern coast of present-day U.S. for The Netherlands; the Dutch then claim parts of New York, New Jersey, Delaware, and Connecticut and name the area New Netherland

1619—Virginia's House of Burgesses, America's first representative lawmaking body, is founded

1619—The first shipment of black slaves arrives in Jamestown

1620—English Pilgrims found Massachusetts' first permanent town at Plymouth

1621—Massachusetts Pilgrims and Indians hold the famous first Thanksgiving feast in colonial America

1622—Indians kill 347 settlers in Virginia

1623—Colonization of New Hampshire is begun by the English

1624—Colonization of present-day New York State is begun by the Dutch at Fort Orange (Albany)

1625—The Dutch start building New Amsterdam (now New York City)

1630—The town of Boston, Massachusetts is founded by the English Puritans

1633—Colonization of Connecticut is begun by the English

1634—Colonization of Maryland is begun by the English

1635—Boston Latin School, the colonies' first public school, is founded

1636—Harvard, the colonies' first college, is founded in Massachusetts

1636—Rhode Island colonization begins when Englishman Roger Williams founds Providence

1638—The colonies' first library is established at Harvard

1638—Delaware colonization begins when Swedish people build Fort Christina at present-day Wilmington

1640—Stephen Daye of Cambridge, Massachusetts prints *The Bay Psalm Book*, the first English-language book published in what is now the U.S.

1643—Swedish settlers begin colonizing Pennsylvania

1647—Massachusetts forms the first public school system in the colonies

1650—North Carolina is colonized by Virginia settlers in about this year

1650—Population of colonial U.S. is about 50,000

1660—New Jersey colonization is begun by the Dutch at present-day Jersey City

1670—South Carolina colonization is begun by the English near Charleston

1673—Jacques Marquette and Louis Jolliet explore the upper Mississippi River for France

1675-76—New England colonists beat Indians in King Philip's War

1682—Philadelphia, Pennsylvania is settled

1682—La Salle explores Mississippi River all the way to its mouth in Louisiana and claims the whole Mississippi Valley for France

1693—College of William and Mary is founded in Williamsburg, Virginia

1700—Colonial population is about 250,000

1704—*The Boston News-Letter*, the first successful newspaper in the colonies, is founded

1706—Benjamin Franklin is born in Boston

1732—George Washington, future first president of the United States, is born in Virginia

1733—English begin colonizing Georgia, their thirteenth colony in what is now the United States

1735—John Adams, future second president, is born in Massachusetts

1743—Thomas Jefferson, future third president, is born in Virginia

1750—Colonial population is about 1,200,000

1754—France and England begin fighting the French and Indian War over North American lands

1763—England, victorious in the war, gains Canada and most other French lands east of the Mississippi River

1764—British pass Sugar Act to gain tax money from the colonists

1765—British pass the Stamp Act, which the colonists despise; colonists then hold the Stamp Act Congress in New York City

1766—British repeal the Stamp Act

1770—British soldiers kill five Americans in the "Boston Massacre"

1773—Colonists dump British tea into Boston Harbor at the "Boston Tea Party"

1774—British close up port of Boston to punish the city for the tea party

1774—Delegates from all the colonies but Georgia meet in Philadelphia at the First Continental Congress

1775—April 19: Revolutionary war begins at Lexington and Concord, Massachusetts

     May 10: Second Continental Congress convenes in Philadelphia

     June 17: Colonists inflict heavy losses on British but lose Battle of Bunker Hill near Boston

     July 3: George Washington takes command of Continental army

1776—March 17: Washington's troops force the British out of Boston in the first major American win of the war

May 4: Rhode Island is first colony to declare itself independent of Britain

July 4: Declaration of Independence is adopted

December 26: Washington's forces win Battle of Trenton (New Jersey)

1777—January 3: Americans win at Princeton, New Jersey

August 16: Americans win Battle of Bennington at New York-Vermont border

September 11: British win Battle of Brandywine Creek near Philadelphia

September 26: British capture Philadelphia

October 4: British win Battle of Germantown near Philadelphia

October 17: About 5,000 British troops surrender at Battle of Saratoga in New York

December 19: American army goes into winter quarters at Valley Forge, Pennsylvania, where more than 3,000 of them die by spring

1778—February 6: France joins the American side

July 4: American George Rogers Clark captures Kaskaskia, Illinois from the British

1779—February 23-25: George Rogers Clark captures Vincennes in Indiana

September 23: American John Paul Jones captures British ship *Serapis*

1780—May 12: British take Charleston, South Carolina

August 16: British badly defeat Americans at Camden, South Carolina

October 7: Americans defeat British at Kings Mountain, South Carolina

1781—January 17: Americans win battle at Cowpens, South Carolina

March 1: Articles of Confederation go into effect as laws of the United States

March 15: British suffer heavy losses at Battle of Guilford Courthouse in North Carolina; British then give up most of North Carolina

October 19: British army under Charles Cornwallis surrenders at Yorktown, Virginia as major revolutionary war fighting ends

1783—September 3: United States officially wins Revolution as the United States and Great Britain sign Treaty of Paris

November 25: Last British troops leave New York City

1787—On December 7, Delaware becomes the first state by approving the U.S. Constitution

1788—On June 21, New Hampshire becomes the ninth state when it approves the U.S. Constitution; with nine states having approved it, the Constitution goes into effect as the law of the United States

1789—On April 30, George Washington is inaugurated as first president of the United States

1790—On May 29, Rhode Island becomes the last of the original thirteen colonies to become a state

1791—U.S. Bill of Rights goes into effect on December 15

INDEX- *Page numbers in boldface type indicate illustrations.*

About the Author

Dennis Fradin attended Northwestern University on a partial creative scholarship and was graduated in 1967. He has published stories and articles in such places as *Ingenue*, *The Saturday Evening Post*, *Scholastic*, *Chicago*, *Oui*, and *National Humane Review*. His previous books include the Young People's Stories of Our States series for Childrens Press, and *Bad Luck Tony* for Prentice-Hall. In the True Book series Dennis has written about astronomy, farming, comets, archaeology, movies, space colonies, the space lab, explorers, and pioneers. He is married and the father of three children.
